TALES
OF THE TATRAS

KAZIMIERZ P. TETMAJER

TALES
OF THE TATRAS

FOREWORD BY **Carl Carmer**

ROY, PUBLISHERS, NEW YORK

Translated from the Polish by

H. E. KENNEDY AND ZOFIA UMINSKA

Drawings by

JANINA KONARSKA

Initials by

T. ZARNOVER

PRINTED AND BOUND IN THE U. S. A. BY
KINGSPORT PRESS, INC., KINGSPORT, TENN.

FOREWORD

THE SPRINGS that feed the stream of a people's imagination are few and very clear. The numberless, nameless men and women who, without conscious artistry, make the songs and tales of a region are moved to expression by impulses as old as the history of local human habitation.

For a river sings a song which the boys and girls who wander its reaches will never forget, and a desert's awful humming is always in the ears of those who were born there even though they spend long years and die among the whispering grassy hills.

Work, too, feeds the mind with imaginings—the kind of work that the landscape breeds, whether it is the swinging of axes in the woods, the herding of cattle on treeless pastures, the digging of ditches to bring water to parched earth.

And the daily happenstances of a people's life —the true dramas that are played only to the limited audience of a countryside take firm hold on the mind and live long after the players are only names on headstones.

The experiences I have listed above as spurs to the popular imagination are so all-inclusive that many a shrewd and ambitious charlatan would conceal them. He would, for his own aggrandizement,

[5]

have those who follow him believe that a people living in a different part of the world is, through that very fact, strange and inexplicable and menacing. He would destroy anyone who denied this, anyone who tried to show that common experiences bind men together.

The man who put the tales and songs that are printed here into words of his own choosing was a victim of such a charlatan. His starved, lifeless, 75-year-old body was found among the ruins of Warsaw one pitilessly cold afternoon just before the dark year of 1941 was born.

But the death of the body of a poet never accomplishes all that the German charlatan, Adolf Hitler, believes it will. If he were sane, by this time he would have learned his lesson, but his diseased mind still sticks to its old formula—that death puts an end to all things.

This book is ample refutation of the madman's logic. Once Kazimierz Przerwa-Tetmajer was a young poet to whom the people of Poland gave their whole-hearted affection. He returned their love when he grew older by setting down for them the tales and songs of the people of the Tatras, the mountains that towered above his birthplace in northern Poland.

The sky-reaching peaks of the Carpathians that lie between Slovakia and Poland had much to say to the sensitive, imaginative boy who lived at their foot. Their moods are reflected in his recordings of the imaginative flights of his own people.

We Americans have our mountains, too, and we understand. We welcome these tales to our own fire-sides, for we know others like them that are the product of our love for our own hills and valleys.

Like the people of the Tatras, the Indians who lived among our Catskills long ago dreamed that the old moon disappears only to be cut up into more stars to decorate our mountain peaks. Like the Polish mountaineers who told Tetmajer the story of the fearful bear "He" we have our tale of "The Great Bear of Arkansas." We, too, can tell of lost loves, of bold outlaws, of great fights. Time and again we match tale for tale until, on having finished the reading of the book, we feel that we have had a happy, rich, friendly evening beside the leaping flames of an open fire.

This is a book that Americans can take to their hearts. And of all the tales in it perhaps that of Zwyrtala the Fiddler best sums up why this is so. For Zwyrtala died and went to Heaven and soon had the place so disorganized with his fiddling that the angel choir was singing wicked fiddle tunes rather too well. The only solution was for the Management to send him back down the Milky Way into the heart of the Tatras where he is still fiddling.

That is the possibility the German charlatan always forgets. He has murdered millions of Poles but the fiddling of Zwyrtala still mocks him, the tales of the starved Tetmajer still prove him a fool. We Americans know this and are happy that it is so. Our country has its fiddlers and poets, too.

CARL CARMER

CONTENTS

1.

FAR-OFF MARYSIA

ASIEK MOSIENZNY played beautifully on the fiddle, and he knew how to make up songs, such as none could make for miles around. Because of his playing and singing his name resounded far and wide, and folk knew him in Marushyn and in Kraushov, in Dzianish and in Koscieliska Valley. And since women took to men of whom a fame goes round the world (as it used to be said: "What shines bright is woman's delight"), the girls clave to him, and it was well if none of the married women wore out their eyes, they stared at him so. He had no great objection to all that, as men usually haven't, but, for the most part, he paid little attention to it. There were very rich girls, too, who wanted him to marry them, but he didn't bother about them at all, though he had nothing himself except what he got by playing on his fiddle at a wedding, or in an inn, or what he earned at carpentering, at the sawmills or at joinery—he could turn his hand to anything.

But such is the nature of those music-folk— what he didn't care about, give it to him and he wouldn't take it—what he liked he'd give his soul for, even to the devil. There's nothing to be done with such folk as that—they're just stupid!

Jasiek Mosienzny's native village saw but little of him. He wandered continually, especially in summer when the sheep had been driven out to pasture. Folk might meet him in Panschytza, where the Poronin men grazed their sheep, and at the Caterpillar Lakes near Zakopane, or again near Mientushany and Chocholovska Valley, and in Zuberska near Oravtse. Folk knew him everywhere. He came, he played, he taught them new songs—and whithersoever he came at once the girls, aye and even the wedded women, kissed him, and that not on the face but on the hands, and they knelt before him as before a holy picture. Such luck had he! But he mostly rather laughed at it all, and though at times he ran a good bit after that sort of thing, none knew the tune that his heart was playing. . . .

But when he was alone so that none heard him, high up among the peaks or deep in the forest, he would take his fiddle from under his arm and would play and sing to himself in his own way, a different one from the way folk sing in the mountain villages of Rocky Podhale—and his song was something like this:

> *Up among the peaks I'm roving—*
> *Play, my fiddle, play!*
> *Down below the country's spreading,*
> *Far and far away.*

Far and far my gaze is roaming—
(Sound, my fiddle, sound!)
I would take my heart and hold it
With my two hands round.

I would take my heart and cast it—
(Sound, my fiddle, there!)
To the feet of one fair maiden,
If I knew but where.

I would cast it to that maiden—
(Play, my fiddle, play!)
But she ne'er her face will show me,
Hiding far away

I would cast it though 'twere breaking
(Music, softly die!)
At her feet and at her's only
Who will please mine eye.

But mine eyes can nowhere see her—
(Play, my fiddle, play!)
Though across the plain they're gazing,
Far and far away.

It was a bit like that, Jas's song.

And then he got acquainted with Marysia Chocholovska from Koscieliska Valley, who grazed cattle near the Ornak Mountain.

And that Marysia Chocholovska was very

strange, and nobody had ever seen another wench like her. Sometimes she would sit down on a stone or on a tree stump, and would gaze and gaze and stay like that for half a day; at home in the living-room or sitting outside the cottage it was quite the same. She had misty, blue eyes that seemed to look around her, but it was quite plain that she saw nothing in the world. If you spoke to her she would look up at once and would smile, and would talk in such a sweet, pleasant way that her words were like honey dripping into your heart. She would go to dances and weddings, she would even laugh with the lads, but it was clear that she wasn't thinking of all that—her thoughts were other-where; and she liked best of all to sit alone some-where with the cows or shut up in her bedroom at home. Then she would lie down on the grass or on her bed, and would close her eyes and be still. Folk called her "far-off Marysia," for she had gone, as it were, somewhere far away from the world.

But there were those who would have wedded her, for she was a comely maid, just like a flower, a good housewife, modest and well-off. She thanked them for their offers and refused.

"Ask me to your wedding with someone else," she would say, "and I'll ask you to my funeral," and she would smile as sadly as a fading herb and as brightly as water in a mountain torrent.

[16]

She was twenty-three and still it was so.

Oh, and when Jasiek Mosienzny, the music-man, met her near Ornak he went no more that summer to Poronin or Panschytza or to the Zuber Valley. He stayed in Koscieliska, sitting and singing to himself most of the time.

Comfort I can't reap, my maid, to sow it I've neglected.
Comfort bring to me, my Mary, whence 'tis least expected.

Thus he would sing and would look at that Marysia Chocholovska, and whenever she looked back at him his fiddle would quiver in his hand as if his fingers were frozen.

Seeing this, one herd-maiden said to another:

"There! That Jasiek of ours has gone and fallen in love with far-off Marysia. God pity him!"

And jealousy seized them, for a wench is such a rogue that sometimes, even if she doesn't want a man for herself, she will be jealous of another maid. There are a few who aren't like that—but very few.

And that Marysia seemed not to dislike Mosienzny: on the contrary, it would appear sometimes as if she even liked him well enough. But how much of that liking there was he couldn't make out. She talked to him, when he played she listened, sometimes she even asked him to play, and sometimes she would whisper very softly: "Play to me about that Janitzek that grazed cattle. . . ."

Then he would play the tune—you all know it:

Once when I grazing cattle near a wood so green and gay,
Came to me a comely maiden, asked me what I did that way.

He played . . . sometimes he played the same thing for an hour or two without changing, and she listened, getting paler and paler; and then she would say, "Thank you," to him, and would go away and hide herself so well that nobody could find her.

"Oh, Jas, you won't play Marysia to you!" said the wenches to him.

"Even so, I'd rather play to her than kiss you," answered he.

"Oh, Jas, 'tis a pity for you!"

"Though I died for her 'twere no pity."

" 'Tisn't your fate to get her."

"The Lord of Heaven Himself was once miraculously changed."

And then when he went and threw himself down under a fir-tree, with his face to the earth . . . why, 'twas pitiful to see him.

Simon Tyrala, the old shepherd, son of Stanislas —a wise fellow, for he had even been a corporal in

the Austrian Empress Tess's army, in the dragoons
—once said, as he looked at Jasiek the music-man
lying under a fir-tree:

"Those music-men—they're somehow quite
different from anyone else. . . . There are some
of them wise, but a very few, and if you come
across a stupid one it's the very devil!

"There was one in our regiment, in the third
squadron, a trumpeter, a fine fellow. Wait . . .
he had a queer kind of name . . . Niedopil or
something like that, and his Christian name was
Charles; and what do you think he did, when he
fell in love with a wench, a servant-girl in Vienna?
Splash he went into the Danube from a bridge!"

"Goodness gracious!" cried Antosia, Mardula's
daughter, who had just begun her seventeenth
year. "And did he drown himself?"

"They dragged him out scarcely alive, and the
sergeant-major asked him why he was so stupid,
and he says, says he: 'Because a wench I fell in
love with didn't want me.' "

"And what happened afterwards, godfather?"

"As soon as they let him out of the hospital,
splash he went a second time, but that time he managed better for they found him no more."

"Oh, Lord Jesus!"

"And he could play, he could, so well that the
Austrian Field Marshal Laudon himself once gave

him two silver thalers at the maneuvers. He even looked a little like Jasiek Mosienzny about the eyes."

"Oh, I wish somebody would love me like that, too," said Antosia.

Day followed day and week followed week and nothing changed. Far-off Marysia listened to Jas's music, but he got no nearer to her.

"Well, ask her, anyhow," said the wenches, "whether she likes you or not."

"But I daren't."

"Take heart of grace! You're a man, aren't you?"

"And if she says 'no' to me?"

"You'll turn to another."

"God forbid! I'd rather sink into the earth here and now."

"Don't blaspheme."

"Oh, Heaven's not fair to me nor hell terrible."

"Are you so much in love with her?"

But to that question he answered nothing.

And so it remained till one sunny day came, such clear, bright weather as hadn't been yet that year. Jasiek Mosienzny got up early, lifted up his head, looked round at the sky, at the crags, and said to himself:

"True! Am I not a man? Let it be once for all either one way or the other!"

And he went straight to Marysia. He found her standing bent over a stream, her skirt tucked in between her knees, her legs bare to the knee. She was washing.

"Marysh!" says he.

Marysia straightened herself.

"What?"

"Marysh, I can hold back no longer. I love you."

She went red and then very pale.

"I love you," repeated Jasiek. "I'd take you for my wife."

But she shook her head sadly, meaning "no."

"No?" says he, and one could see that it went dark before his eyes.

"No."

"Never?"

"Never!"

"Is that your last word?"

" 'Tis my last."

He could scarcely speak: "Why? I love you like the power of God."

"I'll stay as I am . . . forever. . . . I'll be no man's wife . . . ever."

She turned from him, bent down and began to wash again.

Jasiek Mosienzny tried to speak to her again, but she made him no answer. Tears came and came to his eyes, though he wasn't one to weep. He kept them back from coming on to his cheeks, but it seemed to him that they all dripped into his heart, like the molten tin he'd seen dripping in the casting-house at Forge Valley.

He went away.

But after that far-off Marysia was quite different to him. She avoided him, she sometimes said disagreeable things to him, she never asked him to play, she never listened when he played. It was as if he had done her some wrong—cold, as from ice, wafted from her.

And this tormented that unhappy Jas, for what had he done? He had said he loved her. Had he forced her to love him? Had he intruded on her? No! At one word from her he had stood off from her like as when a thunderbolt strikes a big branch from a fir. She'd refused him. He'd gone away.

And he thought and thought—what could the reason of it be? For that he did not please her? Well, that might be! But that she should never want to wed, she, such a pretty, healthy young girl, was incomprehensible. . . .

Some reason, some reason there must be . . . perchance some heavy grief.

'Tis not for nothing that folk sing:

Mother, though nought pains me, I shall soon be dying.
That I cannot have for which my heart is crying.

[22]

He was so miserable that he didn't know what to do with himself.

"There!" he said to himself, "I wish I hadn't said a word. . . . What have I done to her? Why, I didn't offend her! Why, I didn't insult her! My beloved!"

And he did nothing but walk about somewhere in the forest and play. He played in such a way that once Antosia Mardula, who was herding cows, was so moved by his playing that she wept both loud and long.

"What're you crying for, girl?" asked old Simon Tyrala of her.

"Because Ja . . . Jasiek plays . . . like that . . . godfather."

"Let him play there! Let him play!"

"But . . . I'm so sorry . . . I . . . don't know what to do."

"And why are you sorry?"

"How am I to know . . . godfather?"

As long as the weather was fine Jasiek wandered about the forest with his fiddle and kept up as well as he could. But when the rains came, when the cloudy, gloomy first days of autumn came, when snow powdered the tops of the mountains, when the mist came down and darkened the valleys, his soul for very grief had nearly fled away. For she would not love him, and he knew not how he had offended her, how he had vexed her, what evil he had done. He knew not which was the worst—the first or the second. For her love he would have given his life. For any offense of his he would have atoned with his life . . . he would indeed!

One afternoon Marysia didn't take the cows out. He saw her going into the shepherd's shed where the food was cooked. He went after her. The fire was very low, only just glowing a little. . . . It was darkish.

He said nothing, but sat down on a bench near the wall. She sat on a stool, not looking at him.

Some time passed without a word being spoken. Then Jasiek took his fiddle from the peg on the wall and strummed on the strings with one finger. He ceased; then strummed again, once, twice. Finally, with his fingers, he made his strings sound to the tune:

Once when I was grazing cattle near a wood so green and gay
Came to me a comely maiden, asked me what I did that way.

With that Marysia burst out crying. She stifled it once, but afterwards it burst from her like fire bursts.

Jasiek leaped from his seat: "Marysh, what's the matter? Why are you crying?"

She sobbed on.

"Why're you crying? Your tears are like stones cast at me. Tell me! Why are you angry with me? I can't bear it any longer. What have I done to you? How have I wronged you? Marysh!"

"Oh, you've done nothing to me, you've wronged me in no wise. . . . Only why did you strum that way on the strings?"

Jas fell a-meditating. He thought for a moment, then flung the fiddle to the ground and kicked it. He took Marysia's hands and kissed them.

"Forgive me!" he said.

"I've nothing to forgive. How are you to blame? Not a bit!" answered she.

"Why did you get angry with me?"

"I didn't get angry, Jas, I didn't. . . . You'll never understand it . . . never . . . never!"

"You didn't get angry?" cried Jasiek, looking up at her.

"No, only my heart was full of grief."

Once again tears began to make their way towards Jasiek Mosienzny's eyes, but he kept them back.

"Why was it full of grief?" he asked.

"Oh, if you knew. . . . I've sorrowed . . . in silence . . . and now . . . out loud."

"Was it my fault? . . ."

But tears burst forth again from Marysia's eyes and, heedless now of everything, she began to sob, lamenting thus: "Oh, I loved him, I loved him! . . . Oh, I loved him, I loved him!" and she swayed as if she would faint. She could scarce support herself against the wall, and Jasiek held her up.

"He sang like that while his horses grazed. . . ."

She could say no more; she fell silent, and Jasiek Mosienzny kept kissing her hands and her knees. There was no movement in the mountain shed . . . except a blue flame dancing over the burnt-out ashes where the fire had been.

"He didn't want me," said Marysia after a while. "He married Zosia Tsayovna. I never said a word to him, but he knew that I was perishing. . . . Oh, when the marriage procession went to Chocholov church . . . oh! when it went! . . ."

"Marysh!"

"Nothing. . . . I'll hold it back. . . . They were led to the altar. . . . I stood there—aside. . . . When the priest bound their hands together. . . ."

"Marysh!"

"Nothing. . . . The priest bound their hands together, they exchanged rings, he wedded them, took their oaths . . . and my lad was hers. . . . He came out of the church with a feather in his hat, with red ribbons on his cape. . . . She wore a wreath. . . . Oh, Jasiek! . . . You might live to a hundred and not live through what I did then."

"Marysh!"

"And I stayed so. I stayed there near the church, by the wall. None saw me. . . . They drove off . . . and they played his own tune for him—that same. . . . I stayed there till next morning. . . . I prayed to God to send me death—but death came not. . . . And I vowed to myself and swore an oath: As the priest joined your hands and bound you together forever, so do I vow and swear to Thee, oh God, since Thou hast not deigned to give me this happiness, I will never be led to the altar in a wreath, never, never! I'll be laid in my coffin a maiden as I am."

"Marysh!"

"And he drove off with her to where he'd taken her from—to Dlugopol. There they live; I've seen him time and again since, most often at Ludzimir, at pardons, for they're always there since 'tis near them, in their parish. I go there on purpose . . . four years now . . . and I'll keep going there. . . ."

"Doesn't it hurt you?"

"Aye, but at least I see him. . . . They have children . . . two . . . with gray eyes like his. . . . I saw them. . . . Though they were her children, I would have kissed those gray eyes of theirs. . . . Oh, Jasiek!"

"Oh, Marysh!"

"And so I shall stay forever, alone with that pain."

"And what'll become of us now?"

"Go away, leave me," said Marysia. "You'll find another girl. No luck grows for anyone near me. Such is my cursed fate."

"There—so that was the ice-breath that wafted from you! Do you like me? Even a little bit?"

She took his hands in hers and pressed them with her fingers, and drew them up to her breast and said: "I do like you. I like you very much."

And she tore herself away and ran out of the shed.

And Jasiek stayed, and didn't move till the shepherds came and found him there, looking like a dead man.

"What's the matter with you, Jasiek?" they asked . . . but he said no word, and went out of the shed.

He sought Marysia and found her in the cow-house, milking the cows. A fire-pot glowed beside her.

"Marysh," said Jasiek, "I won't leave you thus, I don't want to. I'm not a fellow that'd dispute with you, or try to take you by force. If you were poor and I rich! But as it is, if you don't care for me, what use am I to you? What is my fiddle to you, or the sounding name it has in the world? I'd throw it down at your feet and my bleeding heart with it and that heartfelt love of mine. But I won't leave you so, or say farewell like this. You're like a saint to me, you're as if you'd stepped down to me from among the angels. I'm alone in the world, like that dry maple tree at Jarzombtre, in the clearing. I've nobody anywhere. I play to the folk and only the wind of the mountains plays to my heart. Be as a sister to me!"

He bent towards her knees, he embraced them, and she put down the milk pail and put her hand on his head, and said: "I can't be anything to anyone now—I want nothing but death. Let us part. Go otherwhere. Leave me alone with that pain in my heart."

"Oh, Marysh, Marysh!" said he. "God's my witness, I'd take that wound to myself, if only 'twere better with you—were well."

"Go! I care for nothing in the world but death."

She gave him her hand and then she pushed him gently towards the door. Jasiek Mosienzny was giddy and something broke in his breast.

He went on and on through the forest, towards Tomanova Crags, not knowing whither he went. When at last he sat down under a red fir-tree, up above the forest, it was quite dark and snow was blowing in the wind and mist had covered the mountains. He took out his fiddle from under his cape, looked at it and said: "Oh, fiddle, what have you given me in my life? What have you played to me? What I don't care for pushes itself into my hands, and what I'd give my soul for isn't mine. . . . What use are you to me when you can't play happiness to me? What good is my sounding name to me? Oh, fiddle of mine!"

He drew his bow across the strings, though a snowstorm from the peaks was coming on, and he sang thus to his playing:

> *Far among the folk I'm faring—*
> *(Play, my fiddle, play!)*
> *Fast within my heart is dying*
> *But my life will stay.*
>
> *Fast within my heart is dying—*
> *(Fiddle, sound to me!)*
> *God for me no joy is sowing—*
> *No joy shall I see.*
>
> *God for me no joy is sowing—*
> *(Fly, my swift bow, fly!)*
> *And thou Marysh, loved, my Marysh,*
> *Of thy sorrow die!*
>
> *Die of pain and die of sorrow—*
> *(Play, my fiddle, play!)*
> *In a green grave thoul't be buried*
> *With thy pain one day.*

So Jasiek Mosienzny the music-man understood Marysia's vow, and it seemed to him as if he were looking down a dreadful precipice, into a bottomless abyss. "O, that was the ice-wind that blew from you," he repeated to himself, and it seemed to him as if at the thought of it all, the very earth would sink from beneath his feet with sorrow for Marysia and for his own love.

"It might have been well with us," he thought; and it seemed to him as if he heard Marysia—far-off Marysia—lying face downward on her bed in the shed—murmur:

"Oh heart! Oh heart! Oh heart! Oh heart!"

2.

THE DEPARTURE OF JACOB ZYCH

NE fine morning in December Jacob Zych said to his wife Katherine, maiden name Zeglen, of the Janik clan:

"Till today I've lived and today I shall die."

That was at Vitov.

When he said that to his wife, she replied:

"Oh, poor soul, poor soul!"

And she sighed.

"Kate," continued Jacob Zych, "I've lived a good deal more than ninety years—perhaps three or five more."

She sighed again.

"And you must be nearly eighty. You were but seventeen when I married you and I was thirty—not much less or more."

"Oh, poor soul, poor soul!"

"You didn't want to be my wife, for I was old."

"Dear, dear, Lord!"

"But they made you, because I was rich."

"Dear, dear, Lord!"

"You cried."

"Dear, dear!"

" 'Twas well if your father and mother didn't beat you."

"Dear, dear!"

"You were an only child and not poor. That seemed a lot to you."

"Oh Lord! 'Twas long ago . . . long ago!"

"But I said: 'If you give me Kate I'll pay your whole debt to the Janik clan, and if not I'll set fire to your cottage.' For I had money."

"Dear, dear!"

"I'd money still that my grandfather Simon left me, who stole it from the chest of a church in Hungary and brought some more back of his own from there."

"Dear, dear!"

"Strong I was and clever. I should have set fire to it as sure as the Bible."

"Dear, dear!"

"And so they gave you to me, though I wasn't so young as all that beside you."

"Oh, no, that you weren't!"

"And you had your eye on Jozek Hucianski, that let himself be crushed by a tree afterwards in the forest from heartbreak."

"Dear, dear!"

"He was young, he was but twenty, he was comely."

"Dear, dear!"

"Do you know how long ago that was?"

"Well?"

"Three score and three or five."

"Dear, dear Lord!"

At noon Jacob Zych only drank a little milk, and then he lay down on the bedding for good and all.

His crony (but much younger than he), Francis Gombos, came to him.

"May the Lord be praised! How's all with you?" he said, entering. "Folk say, friend, that you'll be dying."

"Forever and ever! Welcome, gossip," answered Zych from the bed. "Folk say truly."

"Have you been given a sign?"

"I feel so since morn, since I woke. Be seated, please!"

"Well, it must be so. You today, I tomorrow."

"Oh, truly, it must, it must be so."

"Did you get to feel it yesterday?"

"Yesterday? No. Only this morning, as soon as I woke, dawn hadn't come yet, I knew at once she's not far off—death!"

"Not far off . . ."

"It can't be helped. . . . I've lived long."

"A long time. Few live so long now."

"Few today, but before there used to be such as passed a hundred years, enough of them."

"Bah, before it wasn't like 'tis now."

"Of course not! They didn't work hard and the potatoes didn't rot. At twenty, one still grazed cows and wore a long smock—a boy! Why shouldn't such folk live long? Eh?"

"That's so, that's so," assented Glombos. "Nobody made breeches for a fellow till he married. Nobody here ever knew aught of doctors then. None died but those that were bound to. Not like now. . . ."

"That's so, that's so!"

"Everything was different. A cart! If you gave at most eighteen crowns for a cart, there, it outlived you! Truly it did. There were no wedges in it, no iron round the wheels; but folk didn't go far off, so it lasted."

"It did, it did!"

"None sought grease for it. It went along, and if it began to squeak they pushed a mushroom into the wheel and it went on."

"Why wouldn't it? Truly, it went on."

"Things used to be different. Take a christening. At the worst, the old women christened with water and 'twas all right. For there wasn't much either, of this going to church. No, though folk went sometimes. When it was winter and the frost was sharp and none could enter a cottage where there was an unchristened babe, for the fairies would ride its godmother into a heap of snow. You couldn't leave it in the belfry, either, for the fairies would see it there, too; so the godfather would strike the blade of his axe into the wood at the corner of the church and hang on it the sack with the babe in it. Before 'twas written down in there, before the sexton had put on his boots and the priest his vestments, the babe at the corner slept sound enough—it froze."

"Aye, aye, 'twas so!"

"But none made much ado about it, after all. Folk would be a bit sorry if 'twas a boy and had long fingers, for it would have been good for a shepherd, to milk the sheep and play the horn."

"Heigh ho!"

"They would give the priest two shiny coins. He would sing and say a prayer. Hey, then they would bury it and go home."

"Hm, hm!"

"It was altogether different before. One gave, on the Dry Mountain, two shining coins for a pound of salt—but it *was* a pound. Nobody weighed it there on the scales or skimped it. It was a pound! The scales were of wood. At one end there was a weight, hey, as big as a head! That was a pound!"

"Heigh ho! It used to be like that before, long ago. Aye."

"Bah, but those times are gone."

In the afternoon Jacob Zych got weaker. Old

Tylkula, the witch woman, came. It seems she was older still than Zych himself. Zych's wife brought her. She sat down before the hearth. She began to throw burning charcoal in the form of a cross into a basin full of water from nine springs. Zych looked on quietly from his bed.

"Did it let you go somewhat?" asked his wife.

"Why should it let me go? Why, her enchantments won't take away five years nor fifteen. I never was ill and so I shan't die of illness, only of old age. Give the woman some linen and fat bacon for having danced round with charcoal near the stove for nothing."

"And what if we sent for the priest at Chocholov?"

"No, I don't need him. Why should I talk with the farm-hand when I shall soon talk with the Master Himself? But He's not such an one as Jozek Smas from Olcha thought (I was his comrade), —the same in Heaven as Smas at Olcha. When they started, time and again, he and Sam Voytek from Zakopane, to dispute as to what that Farm up there would be like, with the sun of gold and the moon of silver and the stars for money scattered about: there was something to listen to, for those were good talkers, pleasant fellows. Only they were such people for tales! They used to say when the moon grew less and there were more stars, that it got smaller because God in Heaven was making stars; 'minting money' they used to say! And when it got bigger they would say that the angels had dug out some ore and brought it there. Such dream-makers they were! How I laughed at them sometimes! . . . Man thinks himself the lord of all creatures, of cattle and wild beasts and likes to command, so he thinks that the Lord God does no work, only rules."

"For it's true, Gossip," remarked Gombos with conviction. "The Lord God rules. . . . He rules! The Lord God reigns. . . . He reigns!"

"That He reigns I know," said Jacob Zych, "but not like folk think. If it angers someone that some Bartek hit somebody, it must annoy the Lord God, too! Stuff and nonsense!"

"Maybe you think there are no sins?" said Gossip Gombos, contradictorily.

"There are," answered Zych.

"God's judgment is terrible," said Gombos.

"Terrible—that's true," retorted Zych. "The sky will bow down and the earth will creak. The angels will play on horns and the mountains and the pastures will fall in pieces at the sound. Then, never fear, nobody will escape and nobody will wriggle out. But the Lord God is wise. He knows that if a man did wickedly, not for ten or fifteen years but for fifty or a hundred, that hundred years is not eternity. The Tylko chimneys are not the Spiz Peak. I fear purgatory, not hell."

Gossip Gombos said cautiously, but from his own inmost judgment, knowing that his thought would not be finally contradicted:

"You say, Gossip, that you don't fear hell. How's that? Does it mean that there isn't any, or what? But where could the devils stay if it weren't there? And devils you know there are."

"There are," answered Zych, "and all kinds of them. There are Beelzebubs, Ashtaroths, demons; there are field devils, wood devils, house devils, tempting folk. One must chase them away with the Holy Cross, for they fear it. They lie in wait for folk everywhere. Even here in this room there are plenty of them—perhaps a hundred and perhaps a thousand."

Gossip Gombos shivered and Zych's wife whispered:

"Lord, defend us! Sweetest Lord Jesus save us! Holy Virgin!"

Zych continued: "Devils tempt and torment. They're terribly wicked and determined, that's quite true, for from the creation of the world they've been trying to drag some human soul to hell, and till now they've never dragged one there and never will, for the Lord God's wisdom will prevent them!"

Gossip Gombos and Zych's wife fell silent.

Later Zych's children, grandchildren and great-grandchildren, those of them who were on the spot and not away somewhere in the world, gathered together in his cottage to bid him farewell. He was evidently thinking of something, and from time to time he looked round him at those present as if he were seeking something and choosing among them with his eyes as of a century-old vulture, white with age and fading. Several times he looked round like that, and each time looked the longest at Stashek Koys, son of his youngest daughter, Vikta—his favorite grandson, now a grown boy, handsome, clever, strong and wonderfully bold. Then he said:

"Go out, all of you, and let Vikta's Stashek stay here."

They all went out.

"Stashek, come near me," he said.

Stashek approached his grandfather's bed.

"Listen, child," said Zych. "I've chosen you for I like you best of all, and you seem to me the finest. Are you brave?"

"Why, of course."

"Strong?"

"I'd beat anybody."

"Listen! Near Saint John's chapel near Novy

Targ, when the first sun-ray shows, where the shadow of the chapel first falls on the grass, money lies hidden in a small cauldron, money that I and Joe Smas and Joe and Stash Luscyk and your father's father, Martin Keys, brought from beyond the Tatra Mountains and hid there."

Towards evening it could be seen that Jacob Zych got very weak. Then said he to his wife:

"Come here, old woman."

His wife came near to him.

She bent over and he took her in his arms and kissed her on both cheeks, and she kissed him, too.

"Good-bye, my old woman."

"Oh, Jake, Jake!"

"Oh, Kate!"

"God lead you into eternal life."

"And may He be, Kate, your aid in your last hour!"

"And receive you, Jake, into heavenly glory, Amen!"

"Amen!"

"Amen!"

His children, grandchildren and great-grandchildren, men already old and gray, oldish women gray-haired already; men in the prime of life, women in the flower of their age, some with babes at their breast, youths, growing children, young children and babies, gathered round Zych's bed and he blessed them. Then he said: "Make way!" and stood up by himself. Full dressed he had lain down on the bed, in his sandals and breeches and belt, having thrown off his cape only; he stood up and, leaning on the shoulders of those who surrounded him, went staggering slowly towards the window. He could see thence the Red Summits, the Chimney Crags, the Vitov uplands overgrown with old, red firs, with immemorial forest, and the clearings—great, snow-covered plains. The red sun shone on the mountains like fire and blazed like fire in the frozen sky. Then Zych said:

"The bear sleeps, 'tis time for me, too. Fare ye well, ye crags and pastures!"

He went forward a few steps along by the wall, leaning his hand on it, going towards the shelf on which lay his old robber's knife, with its curved blade and with three brass balls on its hilt. He made three crosses with it in the air and crossed himself with it three times. Then he bent down, supporting himself with his hand on the table, and made with the point on the floor a circle round him. All present had moved away towards the wall. Within that circle he lay down, supporting himself behind with his hands as he lowered himself to the floor, face upwards. He lay there for a moment, closed his eyes, sighed a few times and died.

On the third day he was put in his fir-wood coffin, and with him were put in a pipe, tinder, a very old shirtbrooch and a robbers' picture, painted on glass, which had been his favorite in his life-time.

No procession followed the wooden sledge the coffin was placed on, for the church was far off and the snow deep and soft. The eldest son put sides to a sledge and placed the coffin between them. He put a straw rope round his waist, took a hatchet and an iron fork against the wolves, took his seat on the coffin and was off. He looked well to it that the horse wasn't frightened by wolves and the coffin thrown out so that anything fell from it, for he remembered very well what his dead father had often said: "If you're driving a dead man to his burial, and if folk have put in his coffin the things he liked in his life-time, such as a pipe, snuff, his rosary or any picture, God forbid you should lose aught of his. He'd give you something if you did! He'd stand on a cloud and beat down seven fields with hail. Turn back and search. You must! Let him have his own!"

Thus died Jacob Zych of Vitov, and thus was he taken to his burial.

3.

MARYNA

Maryna the miller's daughter goes down to the mill by the water.
From the mill she's homeward faring, her flour with no man sharing.

HUS folk sang about Maryna, Kruzel's daughter of Rogoznik village. Later on another verse came into use which ran thus:

Maryna the miller's daughter goes glad to the mill by the water,
But Mat the mayor's son meetly taught her to walk there discreetly.

That was later on, though, after the wedding. Mat really did show her how to behave when she walked abroad.

She was a girl whose equal you couldn't easily find in the neighborhood. At Ludzimir at a pardon or in the town or at Black Dunajec at the fair there wasn't a man who wouldn't look at her hard, or a woman who wouldn't stare her through and through. She was tall and straight and held her head high. Her eyebrows were black, as if they had been painted, set high above her eyes. Her forehead was smooth, and she had immense, dark blue eyes. Her nose was straight, her mouth was red and small. Her chin was round. Her hair was black and glossy, as if it had been polished, and so abundant that she could cover herself with it as with a cape. And then there was the color of her face, the sunburnt blush on her swarthy skin, and then there was her slender neck and her bosom boldly outlined beneath her bodice. There was the lovely line of her waist, her figure, supple and full, her whole body, that seemed to be fashioned of soft iron. And her voice! . . . When she sang it seemed that the world would melt. . . . When she walked, even through the greatest crowd, she had no need to say: "Make way!" Everyone who looked at her made way for her.

But even so fate had something in store for her.

The girl was a rich one, proud, bold and disobliging. Her father was the chief man in the village, old Bart Kruzel, whose place had been called "White Martin's" ever since his grandfather's time. He was a widower. He had nobody but her and thought the world of her. He had a holding of about fifty acres, about five acres of woodland, a tremendous great farm and the mill. And that wench Maryna kept watch on the miller's boy the whole time so that nobody should have a chance to steal a grain of flour, and kept continually going back and forwards between the house and the mill till people began to sing songs about that way of hers. But none dared to sing them when her eyes were upon them, for she had eyes like glowing brands, like fire glittering on water. When she looked at a fellow it just went through him. One farm-hand from Ostrovsk who was driving a cart with wine in it when he caught sight of her, leaned back in the cart and went dumb for a moment and just opened his mouth. She smiled and passed on, and then he said:

"Has a she-devil taken woman's form, or what? But if such as she live in hell I'd like to burn there up to my ears!"

Nobody took to her, because of her disobligingness and pride. She was already twenty, but had no wish to be married.

"Maryna, will you never wed?" asked her aunt.

"Is there anyone worthy of me?" she asked in return.

"Dost know," went on her aunt, "what folk sing?"

Why dost thou scorn me, maiden, why dost thou say me nay?
If I don't wed thee, maiden, no noble will come thy way.

"And didn't you hear, aunt, what old Budz was telling, how a king's son came to a wheelwright's daughter?"

"Fairy tales!"

But it came to pass that Jasiek Mosienzny, called the Musician, met her.

It happened thus. He couldn't get over his refusal by Marysia from Chocholov, though several years had passed since they parted—perhaps three. He went no more to Koscieliska Valley, and even ceased to wander through Cold or Rocky Podhale, he even kept more to the low-lying villages and played less but worked more at carpentry and sawing: but when he played it was a hundred times more beautifully than before. It is enough to say that the Hungarian gypsies wanted him to join a troupe of theirs that played even in Buda-Pesth. He refused.

He heard that Gonsiorek of Rogoznik wanted a man to do sawing and carpentry. He took service with him.

Then the wenches and older women of Rogoznik were glad, for they had heard of him (as they had heard of Janicek of old, whose good looks were so famous and who came to a sad end through an unkind maiden) that there was no such music as his in the world. But it was reported of him, too, that all through that three years since he had parted with Marysia he had had no love-affair with any woman. And at Rogoznik, too, he looked at the girls as if they had been daws on a red fir tree. That was all he cared about them!

But that state of things didn't last long. Kuba Gonsiorek of the sawmill said to him one day:

"Look here, Jasiek, take this spring wheat up to White Martin to be ground."

"All right."

Then old Gonsiorek smiled to himself, and asked:

"Have you seen the miller's girl?"

"Which one?"

"The mayor's daughter."

"No."

"Then beware or she'll eat you."

"Oh, if I haven't been eaten till now, even she won't eat me."

"Beware, I tell you! Stephen, son of Simeon from Ludzimir, ran away to Pesth because of her. Kuba Gonsiorek from our own Rogoznik itself is drinking so that there's no hope for him. Vaclav Jahymiak has gone quite stupid—and all because of her."

"I'm not afraid."

"Have you anything with you to save you from bewitchment?"

"I have."

Then old Gonsiorek got terribly curious. He bent his gray head, with its long locks and its plaits hanging down from the temples, towards Jasiek and asked:

"What is it? What? What have you? I won't betray you. Do tell me!"

"Oh, what I have I have. It'd be no good to you."

"Have you got it on you?"

"I always have it."

"Where? In your belt?"

"Maybe so, if my belt were broad enough."

"How can that be? I don't understand."

"Oh, father, 'twould be in my belt if my belt were broad enough to cover my heart. Where's the spring wheat?"

But old Gonsiorek kept looking at him, and asked:

"It's on your heart, is it?"

"Just so."

"How can that be? Is it stuck on? Is it a kind of plaster?"

"It's not stuck on. It has to be swallowed to get down to the heart," said Jasiek.

Old Gonsiorek put his head on one side.

"You're saying queer things," says he. "Will you show it to me? Couldn't I swallow it?"

"Oh, you'd have to go to Koscieliska Valley to see what it's like."

"Is it there?"

"Just so."

"And who gave it to you?"

"Why are you asking so much about it? Where's the wheat?"

Old Gonsiorek was silent for a moment, then he laughed outright, and said:

"You're right. Why do I ask when I have, here on my head, the best safeguard against all kinds of charms"—and he stroked his gray locks.

"Come along, Jasiek," he continued, "and let's put the spring wheat into the sack."

A little while later it was with Jasiek the Musician as if a thunderbolt had struck him.

He went along carrying the sack on his back and came near to the mill, and before it stood Maryna, the miller's daughter.

"Are you coming to the mill?" she asked.

Jasiek looked for a moment at her, and his legs bent under him and his face went white, though he had a good large sack on his back.

For the glance of Maryna's eyes pierced him through and through.

She only smiled a little, a smile that flitted over her thin lips, and she looked at him loftily, boldly, and he just stood before her, bending under his sack.

"Come on!" she said. "We'll take it over to the mill."

Jasiek gave the sack of grain to the miller's lad to be ground.

"You work not far from here?" said Maryna. "You're the music-man, Jasiek, from Gonsiorek's."

"I am." She did not address him as an equal, but spoke to him as she would have spoken to a shepherd, he remarked.

"Come tomorrow morning for the flour," she said.

"All right."

He wanted to say "good-bye," but she looked no more at him, and went away from the mill through the meadow, towards her home.

Jasiek turned to go back.

With that Maryna's voice sounded—the air bore it far and wide:

Lily, lily, how came you here, where the high peaks loom?
In the valleys you grow dear, on the mountains you bloom.

Give me in marriage, mother, while the folk ask for me.
While the lily is blooming it's plucked for its flower, you see.

Give me in marriage, mother, now, ere my beauty pass.
The lily is sweet, my mother, while it blooms in the grass.

Give me in marriage, mother! Like the lily some even-
*   tide*
I'll be blown away by the wind, dear, far over the
*   world so wide.*

Mother, my little mother, and never a bit you'll know
Where did the little lily out of your garden go.

Lovely indeed was the singing—as sweet, as wonderful as if a mother were singing her child to sleep.

Jasiek Mosienzny couldn't conceive how such a kind, caressing voice could come from a wench like that, who looked so arrogant and proud. It pierced his heart through and through, for, you see, he was a musician himself, and he felt it more than others.

He walked on, looking about him, and Maryna glided through the meadows with a yellow kerchief on her head, with white sleeves and a red bodice, and with a red cloak over her dark skirt, the colors shimmering on her like flowers on the meadow, so splendid was she—a very flaming torch! Jasiek kept glancing at her.

And she kept on singing from afar, still more sweetly, still more enchantingly:

Hear Janicek's music through our valleys go—
Like the sheep that wander through the bushes low.

Our Janicek's glory ne'er will die away
In the valleys pleasant, on the mountains grey.

Her voice rang and his heart melted within him.

Come thou boldly, Janicek, when you see in the win-
* dow hay—*
If there's straw in the window, mother's at home to-
* day.*

Jasiek's heart leaped within him.

But she, still singing, disappeared into a willow-grove that grew just by the village.

Jas's heart quivered and he thought to himself: "How could that be? She only just sang like that. Would such a wench think of me? Why, she didn't even deign to look at me!"

In this doubting mood he went towards Gonsiorek's sawmill, and everything in him was a-quiver.

"Well, how went it?" asked Gonsiorek. "Did you give the spring wheat to be ground?"

"I did."

"Did you see the miller's daughter?"

"I did."

"And what then?"

"Nothing."

"Nothing?"

"Nothing."

"Did what you swallowed in the Koscieliska Valley keep you safe?"

"Where are the planks we were to saw?" asked Jasiek.

"Oho!" thought old Gonsiorek, "it defended you nicely if you're in such a hurry for work! Go and drink another pint of that medicine." Aloud he said:

"The planks? The planks are ready, take them. But it seems to me that your hands will shake to-day."

Jasiek answered nothing, and went away to saw the planks.

Old Gonsiorek went to smear the wheels of his cart with black grease, for he intended to go to the fair at Novy Targ.

But as for Jasiek, something was already melting inside him. He cut the planks, he sawed them, and before his eyes was Maryna's beauty and her singing sounded in his ears.

Marysia of Chocholov, far-off Marysia, had been like honey, but this one was like fire. By her singing she had first laid a charm on him and then made advances to him. Why had she done it? It was certain that she hadn't sung as she had done without a reason. She must have seen him some-where in church, someone must have pointed him out to her. . . .

Poor unfortunate Jasiek Mosienzny had a heart of this sort: Three hundred women might hang round his neck at once and he wouldn't say a word, but when he hit on the right one, good-bye to him! There was neither vein nor rib in him—wax!

"I'll be done for through her," thought he.

"If a fellow tried?" he thought again.

"Eh, you may try to get anything out of her, you may!" he said to himself. "It's not your luck."

"I had no luck there in Koscieliska. Perhaps the Lord'll bless me here."

"He didn't bless better men than you."

"Oh, just to see her once more!"

"Why, man, you're going up for the flour to-morrow!"

"And that Marysia over there in Chocholov?"

But the memory of Marysia from Chocholov in Jas's fastidious but artistically sensitive heart had faded suddenly like a picture exposed to the rain.

"The far-off one? Marysia? If only she had wanted me! But she won't wed anyone—ever!"

And that immense word "ever" made Jasiek's inward dissension cease.

That night—it was in July, and fine, starry weather—Jasiek played for a long time on the willow-pipe (for he knew how to play on everything), sitting on the sawing-block in the yard. And old Gonsiorek, lying in his bed, muttered to himself: "Squeak, squeak! You'll squeak louder still, never fear! Already your soul's creeping out of the holes in the willow. Soon it'll be hopping all over your body like a bird on the branches."

Jasiek Mosienzny slept little that night until just before dawn, when he went sound asleep and dreamed that a procession was coming, and in that procession was Marysia of Chocholov, and she turned her face to him—he was standing at the side—and said to him: "Oh, Jas, it's just my cursed fate!"

And she disappeared and something threw him, and it was as if he were falling down a precipice.

Next day he went early to the mill for flour, and as he got nearer he got hotter and hotter.

Maryna was standing in the doorway.

"May the Lord be praised!" said Jasiek, and raised his hat.

"Forever and ever, Amen," said Maryna.

"Is the flour ready?"

"It is so."

She measured it out to him herself. He scarcely dared to look at her, but when he did her eyes were on him, glowing like altar-candles.

"Hey, you've no business here!" he thought to himself.

Then, as he was about to take the sack away, Maryna said to him:

"Jasiek, do you know I've turned away the

horse-boy? Wouldn't you take a job with us?"

"I?"

"You."

"With you?"

"Just so."

He looked at her. She stood before him like the sunrise.

"Would you like to have me—really and truly?"

"Aye indeed! Why should I play a trick on you?"

It went light and dark before Jas's eyes.

"I'll take service with you."

"Then give Gonsiorek notice and move in to us."

"Did you ask the mayor, your dad?"

"Dad does everything I want."

"When can I come?"

"Today, even."

Jasiek went back to the sawmill to tell Gonsiorek he was leaving, and Maryna sat on the threshold of the mill and sang:

Though I look on one lad, though I look on two,
You're not here, Janicek, and I wait for you.

Curs'd is all my loving, curs'd, for all in vain.
You have bound my heart, dear, with a silver chain.

MARYNA

On the mountain meadow, swallow, build your nest.
Heart of mine, take comfort, calm thee, be at rest.

But the little swallow far has flown away
And my heart is mourning ever and a day.

That was the song that followed swiftly after
Jasiek; wistful, tuneful notes sent out into the
world like the branches of the beech-tree, like the
sparkling strands of the spider's web in autumn,
and it flooded Jasiek's soul and confused it, and all
the blood from his hands and feet ran to his heart;
so powerfully did Maryna's song work upon him!

"That wench will eat you," prated old Gonsiorek as he paid Jas for his services.

"Let her eat me now! Do you know what Jano-
shek said when they had tormented him and were
going to hang him? 'As you've roasted me, now
eat me, too!'" answered Jasiek.

Then a strange time began for him.

Maryna, like a king's daughter, busied herself
about the house and the mill, and he kept round
about her like as he would have done round about
a princess. Never a word, never anything! Jasiek
dried up, he couldn't eat, he couldn't sleep. It
seemed to him that he could have her for the taking, but nothing happened.

He had no power over himself, he had attacks

as of the ague, but he felt so shy that he couldn't force himself to advance a step towards Maryna. The words stuck fast in his throat and in his breast.

Until one morning he thought to himself:

"Why should I torment myself here? I'll fling everything to the four winds and go to the devil."

And so he decided.

But it happened that there came a child at dinner-time to Kruzel's, a little, tiny, three-year-old boy belonging to Philomena Komperda, a relative of the mayor's late wife.

"What have you come for?" asked old Kruzel.

"For apples," said the child.

"Do you like me?"

"Yes, I do."

"And do you like that girl?" asked the mayor, pointing to Maryna.

And the little boy said: "I don't like her."

"You don't like me?" asked Maryna.

"I don't like you."

"Not even a bit—a tiny bit?"

"I don't like you."

"Not even that much?" and she showed him the end of her finger and smiled, and spoke with such a lovely, caressing voice that it seemed to Jasiek that the fuchsias on the window-sill bent their flowers towards her to listen.

"Not even that much?"

And the boy reflected, and said: "Just that much."

And Maryna's eyes shone like quiet stars after sunset.

And Jasiek the Music Man stayed and tended the mayor's horses.

"Oh, if you were not what you are, Maryna," he thought, and bit his lip. "If you were not so beautiful, so proud, so rich. Oh, if you were not what you are!"

"Oh, if you were not what you are! If even you were as beautiful and as proud, but not so rich!"

What would she think first of all?—That those fifty acres of ground, those five acres of forest, those horses, those cows, those sheep, that mill, still more than herself, smelt sweet to him. And she would look at him in a way that he couldn't bear.

Old Shymek Tyrala, son of Stash, told the truth when he said that those music men were somehow quite different people, that even though some of them were wonderful and clever, if there happened to be a stupid one, he was the very devil! For anyhow anyone that wanted to marry a girl like Maryna would naturally think first of all about her fortune and only afterwards about her beauty, and nobody would wonder at it, not even she herself. But Jasiek was one of those music men who were not wise.

"If she had been poor. . . . But as it was!"

If any man or woman could have heard him meditating like that they would have said to him:

"Why, you're as stupid as a ram!"

Soon afterwards it happened that Andrew Kruzel, Maryna's uncle, on her father's side, gave his daughter in marriage.

Jasiek played at the wedding, and with him was another fiddler and a double-bass player. The wenches were like roes, like flowers! But what were any of them to Maryna?

Jasiek played, and had eyes for none but for her.

There came to that wedding Mat (son of a former mayor of Rogoznik, Bartholomew Fita). Folk called him "the mayor's Mat" or "the little mayor's little Mat." He had just left the army, the cavalry. He had a red cap on his head, a blue jacket on him; he was a comely lad, graceful, well-built and not poor. When he stamped to a quick-time Rogoznik tune, one saw the sparks fly, though he wore leathern sandals.

He led Maryna out to dance the polka—oh, when they began to go!

He had been abroad, in Vienna, in Pressburg, in Olomunietz. There he had learnt to dance with

Austrian frauleins, with Czech "holkas." He took Maryna round the waist, clasped her to him, carried her through the air.

The company was called to table. It was late at night. Jasiek went out into the field to breathe the fresh air, for he was tired with playing; but that was nothing. His heart was like to break with grief, jealousy, pain and anger. He had sat playing by the wall, he had played till the hairs from his bow flew about and that other had clasped Maryna, that other had carried her and pressed her to his breast!

When he came back "the little Mayor's little Mat" threw him three pence for his fiddling, called a tune and went to dance with the bride. As for Jasiek, he was inclined to dash his fiddle to the earth and jump up and seize Mat by the throat.

But he didn't. . . . He did nothing.

Four weeks hadn't passed when the betrothal of Mat, the little mayor's son, to the miller's Maryna was announced. Jasiek wanted to fling everything away and run to the devil, but Maryna kept saying to him:

"You'll play at my wedding, Jasiek?"

So he stayed on.

Mat kept on coming to Kruzel's day after day, always merry, always smiling, always happy. Once, when Maryna answered her father back arrogantly at supper, Mat said to her: "Do you know, Maryna, if you were ever to answer me back that way, I would smack you so hard that you wouldn't be able to sit down for three days. Remember that!"

Maryna's eyes gleamed. The company happened to be eating sour beet soup. She drew back her hand with the spoon in it, and cried: "I'll hit you on the muzzle, now, here on the very spot!"

And Mat clenched his fist and said: "Hit me!"

But Maryna bent her head and started eating again, and old Kruzel, the miller, said:

"That's the way! Holy Lord, when a woman makes for one with a harrow one should make for her with a flail. When a woman makes for one with a knife one should make for her with a scythe. That's the right way, holy Lord!" This was Kruzel's manner of speech.

But Jasiek's heart died within him.

Towards night he was going through the yard when he saw Maryna sitting on a tree-stump by the cowshed and crying.

"Why are you crying, Maryna?" he asked her tenderly and with awe, for it was the first time he had seen her weeping.

"Because he'll beat me."

"Who?"

"Mat."

"Then don't marry him."

"How can I not when he wants me to?"

"But you can *not* want to."

"I can't."

"Have you fallen in love with him?"

"No, but I'm as if I were charmed."

"*You* are?"

"I am."

Jasiek sat down heavily beside her.

"Maryna, listen!" he said. "Why did you engage me to serve you?"

"Because I liked you."

"Me?"

"You."

"Why do you tell me that now? Oh, sweetest Lord Jesus!"

"I liked you . . . because of the fame that went forth of you through the world. Folk talked of you."

"And now?"

"And now nothing. It's over and done with."

"Over and done with?"

"Forever."

"Why? What for?"

"Because you're as nothing to me."

"Why? I'd have lain at your feet and been as faithful as a dog to you. I'd have looked at you as at a star."

"That's just what I don't like in you—you're soft."

"Is the other better, who will beat you?"

"But he's a man!"

Jasiek Mosienzny grabbed his head in both his hands.

"Maryna!" he cried. " 'Twould have been better not to say that. God's wounds!"

And he rocked his unhappy head to and fro, and a despairing grief possessed him.

Then Maryna said:

"I didn't know. I thought 'Like me he does, but if he loved me he would have made advances to me.' I'm not the kind to stretch out my claws to anyone first"—and she raised her head proudly.

But Jasiek rocked to and fro in his pain. "Hey . . . that's what I should have done . . . and I never knew . . . and what now?"

"It's over and done with."

Suddenly Jasiek jumped up. "And what if I killed him?" he cried.

But Maryna answered: "Then they'd shut you up in prison and hang you, and even if they didn't I'd never be your wife. There's a soft spirit in you —a child's, not a man's."

"What'll happen to us now?"

"Nothing. I've lost the will to be yours. You're soft."

Jasiek stood up.

"Good-bye," he said.

"Oh, no! You must play at my wedding."

"For nothing in the world!"

"Little Jasiek! Why, you like me, don't you? You'll play for me. Don't say nay."

So Jasiek stayed and played.

He played for three days and three nights, for so great a wedding did Kruzel give his daughter. He played so that his strings not only creaked but broke, and he tore a whole new bow to pieces. He played till the skin came off his fingers, till his heel began to get sore from stamping with it, and water streamed from his hair for three days and three nights. He played so that folk wondered at him, and it seemed to him that his spirit had got into his fiddle, and that he was lashing and lashing and lashing it with his bow, and saying to it: "You're soft —soft—soft! A child's spirit, not a man's."

Throughout the three days and nights of Maryna's wedding nothing passed his lips but wine and brandy. He drank and played. Near dawn on the third night the wedding ended, and so did Jasiek's playing.

He said goodbye to none, he wanted to see nobody; he left his things behind him and went in what he stood up in. With his fiddle only under his arm he went his way from Rogoznik.

He met old Gonsiorek, who was walking round his fence and putting in new sticks. He had been at the wedding, too, for a short time, and was glad that his young wife Margaret stayed on there and that he could rest himself without her at home.

Jasiek said not a word and would have passed him by, but old Gonsoriek put a hand on his arm.

"You don't even give me greeting—me, an old man! You don't even say, "The Lord Jesus be praised!" Where are you going to?"

"Away out into the world."

"Away out into the world? Because of that wedding? Didn't I tell you, 'Beware, for she'll eat you?' And she has eaten you, too."

"God be with you!"

"God guide you! . . . There—she's eaten you —that wench has eaten you. But Mat'll know how to deal with her. I took a good look at him. A splendid man! For her a sort of breeches' strap is needed and not a fiddlestring and bow. You're soft."

"God be with you!"

"And with you! Don't be downcast. Perhaps the Lord Jesus saved you from her, for she'd have killed you."

Jasiek was already going down the high road and old Gonsiorek muttered:

"How dreadfully stupid a man can get through

a woman! And he seemed to be a fine lad, sensible and handy at everything, at sawing and with horses and at the mill, and as for playing, he knew it all down to Amen! And *that* made such a hash of him! Love!"

But Jasiek Mosienzny, called the Musician, was passing through forests and woods on his way towards Hungary, and was saying to himself:

"Oh, fool, fool that I was! Oh, fool, fool!"

And then:

"What kind of a spirit is in me? Truly I wonder at it myself. What I don't want pushes itself into my grasp. What I want is not for me, and what ought to be mine I can't catch, can't get hold of! Am I bewitched? I couldn't get Marysia of Chocholov, I wasted myself finely over her—and this one, whom I could have had, I missed! There! Perhaps it was the fiddle that bewitched me. Maybe it's that that has led me to waste my life, maybe it's that that has softened my soul so that a wench can say to me: 'Your soul is not a man's, but a child's. I've no luck with it, no luck! Maybe it's that that has laid a charm on me. . . . If it weren't for the fiddle she wouldn't have hired me for the horses. It was the talk about me . . . because of the talk."

And such wrath with the fiddle took him that he raised it aloft in his hand, and would have smashed it against a tree-stump. . . . But then he remembered that it was all he had in the world. . . . The fiddle he had, and nothing more . . . that, and the glory that it made for him on the earth.

And he tuned up, but played not any of his accustomed tunes nor any mournful one. He struck the strings with his bow, so that they all sounded at once and gave forth the Black Danube March:

Dark as pitch is the night—Fire gleams through the
    trees are falling.
Dark as pitch is the night—Hear evil to evil calling!
In the clearing beneath the firs a fire in the wood is
    glowing—
Do the wild witch-maidens warm them or devils to
    hell-fire going?

"Come thou to us, young brother—our lot thou shalt
    now be sharing,
And if thy fate fall so, to the grave thou shalt swift be
    faring,
And if thy fate fall so, bright gold in thy grasp shall
    shine,
And with every day a mistress—a sweetheart fair shall
    be thine."

"Hey, brothers of mine, to share your fate I am flying.
Maids in the valleys loved—oh, cease ye your useless
    crying!

[74]

Weep not, sisters mine, like flowering apple-trees
   growing—
Weep not, parents grey-headed, over your son that is
   going!

Weep not for me that to steal, to kill I go—
My roof the wood and my couch, grass, brushwood
   low!
If gold falls to my lot I will scatter it far and free.
If the gallows-tree be my fate, why, the wind will play
   with me."

Playing thus, he went forwards toward Hungary, and his own heard of him no more.

Some said that he joined the gypsy troupe that wanted to enlist him before. Others said he was drowned in the Vaga, others that he drank himself to death, and still others that he joined a band of robbers somewhere away in the Siedmiogrod mountains. Nobody knew for certain. All that remained of him was his fame and the song that folk sang of him:

Known is Janicek's fame all over the countryside:
Though he is gone forever, yet will it aye abide.

4.

HE

THE immense, black bear was born and reared in the dark fir-forest beneath the shadow of the Great Peak, in a place where the sun shone only over the tops of the firs, but could not pierce with its rays the tangle of their boughs and branches, beneath which packs of fierce wolves chased the deer or bears forced their way with their powerful heads or the fatal, silent lynx, in his pale, golden coat slid along twisting paths.

On a certain spring day the bear heard sounds he had never heard before. Amazed, he stood at gaze and listened. Those sounds were measured strokes, hard and dull, awakening dry echoes. They moved forwards and upwards from the valley. Ere long the bear's amazed eyes saw men with axes in their hands, hewing off, on the left and the right, branches of the immemorial firs and thus making a long path behind them. There were several of them; they had bows on their backs and arrows in woven reed quivers and bags of food. At their waists were hung slings and bags full of pebbles. The bear looked at them with terrible, angry eyes. He would have liked to rush upon them, to tear them in pieces and scatter them to the four winds, and yet a kind of awe kept him from approaching them. When they began to advance in his direction he gave vent to an angry,

menacing growl, but he retreated into the undergrowth, made his way into its depths and, sitting
down, lifted up his muzzle and sniffed.

A few days later a path had been cut right
through the trees, to the meadow where tall moun-
tain-sorrel grew and burdocks with their broad
leaves, and a host of flowers and herbs that made
the meadow shimmer and glow with blue and yellow and purple and green colors. Thither the men
drove a flock of sheep and a herd of oxen, beside
or behind which came seven big, white, hairy
dogs, that were the size of wolves and looked like
them. These dogs wore spiked collars.

At once the men began to make a shelter of
stones. On the stones they placed branches of trees
and pieces of bark, and on top of all they placed
heavy stones to keep the branches and the bark
from being blown away.

Round about the mountain meadow the forest
grew empty. The stags and the does that had
grazed there dispersed. The wolves drew near in
the undergrowth, lured by the sight of the sheep
and oxen, but they feared the dogs and the ever-
watchful mountaineer herdsmen and shepherds,
who were armed with bows and slings that shot
far, and with sharp axes and knives. But more than
these they feared the fire that blazed day and night
in the shelter, never going out. The wild, bristled

sows that had lived there before, seeking edible roots, led their tribes of little ones far away. Even the bold, nay, often foolhardy and aggressive boars did not come near the meadow.

From high up among the rocks above the two lakes that lay eternally drowsing in the valley, the swift, inquisitive chamois looked down, but they fled with immense leaps when the shepherds and their sheep came higher up among the crags. Only the mountain eagles sometimes rocked on their wide-spreading wings in the middle air, took aim and fell like a thunderbolt on a lamb, which they bore away with them, if a feathered arrow or a stone from a shepherd's sling, or a swift axe thrown by a shepherd, that roared through the air, making mighty leaps and ever going straight to its mark, did not reach them first.

Soon a pen of branches was made for the sheep and other shelters for the shepherds near the first one, forming a shepherds' camp.

From afar off among the knee-timber the bear looked towards the meadow. A tribe of bears, as many as fifteen of them, lived in the Dark Fir Wood. There they grazed, there they multiplied and were reared, thence they made raids on the green oats in the summer and on the golden oats in the autumn that grew in the villages near the Vaga. There they slept the winter through. Some-

times they moved towards the Quiet Peak near
Kopa, towards the Fish Lake and on to the valleys
where their fellows swarmed. They were the sole
and absolute masters of the mountains. The elk,
with his bifurcated antlers, who lived lower down
than they, fled heavily when he merely came
across the traces of their paws. The monstrous bi-
sons with foreheads that were as hard as rock, that
were as strong as a river in spate, did not graze
high up, and fought only with the bears of the valley that dwelt in the lower woods. The old boars,
with their long, gleaming tusks, chattered and
champed their teeth when a bear was near, but,
placing themselves near the edge of the undergrowth, they made ready for defence alone, not
for attack. The wolves, when they went together,
in a pack, and were hungry, could be dangerous
only on a plain, where no tree grew. Besides, they
were starved and bold to the point of madness in
the winter only, when the bear, well covered,
slept soundly.

So there was no rival, and it was love alone that
filled the mountains with the roaring of fighting
males that sounded like contending storms.
Throughout the Dark Fir Wood, nay, perhaps
through all the Tatra Range, there was none more
terrible than the Black Bear. He had sides that
were like tree-trunks, a head as big as a bush, a

black, glossy coat, and when he rose up on his hind legs he looked like a tree. He was the most terrible bear of them all.

And it was he who first killed an ox on the meadow which the herds and shepherds had taken for their own. He killed it in broad daylight, when it had wandered far into the knee-timber. He hit it such a powerful stroke that it fell dead at once with a broken spine, and hadn't even time to bellow. Its loss wasn't even noticed at once. It was only the multitude of eagles, vultures, hawks, falcons and owls above the carrion that led the herds to it, but they found nothing but bones.

Emboldened by success, the bear attacked another ox of the herd. The cattle scattered in a panic, but the dogs ran up barking, and the herds, axe in hand, came after them. The bear ripped up the boldest among the dogs, cast a rock down towards the men, but fled.

Then a struggle began, for other bears, too, tracked the oxen or attacked the sheep. Specially at night the shepherds and the dogs had to keep watch, for the lynxes stole through the undergrowth, and the wolves howled around, answering back the dogs, that foamed from continual barking.

A relentless struggle it was that began with the birds of prey in the air and the beasts of prey on the earth. But the shepherds had recognized by now that the greatest damage was done, the boldest onfalls made, by the big, black bear.

He got furious with the dogs and with the men. Sometimes day after day he couldn't strike down a single ox or make off with a single sheep. Autumn snow fell early, unexpectedly. It was so thick that it covered the bushes where the long-shaped bilberries grew, and broke the red branches of the blackberry bushes and buried the grass. Famine came. Most of the herds and shepherds, with the oxen and some of the sheep, had gone down to the village, promising themselves to return when the snow melted. There remained only a couple of shepherds with a flock of sheep, which were shut up in a pen and fed with hay that had been cut in the summer. Only two dogs remained there.

One dark and frosty night, full of wind and snow, "He" rushed, like a thunderstorm out of the clouds, from the shadows of the forest, fell, like an avalanche started among the rocks, on the meadow, and raced like a mountain torrent from a lake overflowed with rain, towards the camp. The dogs rushed out to meet him, but he never minded them and they only barked from afar. With one leap he crossed the fence of the pen, and fell upon the sheep that were packed close together and bleating despairingly.

Quicker than thought he hit out with his paws, struck at the crowded sheep. He did not stop to drink their blood—he only hit and hit, beating with his paws and striking out behind him. He got wild with fury amid that frightful slaughter. He killed and killed.

The shepherds heard the barking of the dogs and the bleating of the sheep, but they could not run to help. The brands they tore from the fire went out with a hiss in the wet snow that was falling, and they feared to approach in the darkness, while their cries did not frighten the bear away. "He! He!" they repeated in despair, while "He" raged in the pen like a blaze in a barn full of straw and dry grain. When the sheep got through the wooden fence of the pen and, mad with fear, rushed blindly in all directions, the bear began to drink the blood of those that were warmest, to tear slabs of flesh off the dripping fleeces and swallow them. Finally he seized one sheep, and leaping out of the pen made away with it into the forest.

Next day there was weeping and lamenting in the meadow. It was not enough that "He" had killed more than thirty sheep; the wolves had seized upon many more when they scattered, as could be seen from the traces. Many of them couldn't be found at all, and none knew what happened to them. "He" had completely ruined the pen, and with weeping and cursing, with abuse and threats, the shepherds fled to the village, taking with them all the living and whole sheep that they could herd together. They shut up the carcases of the dead sheep in one of the shelters and, having walled it round and about with boulders, they left it till they could return for the skins and meat. But "He" was on the watch. That very same night he fell, with his comrades, upon the shelter; they tore the boulders away, they swept down the defences, and they feasted there in such wise that the valley was strewn with bloody strips of fleece; and when, three days later, the weather grew warmer and the herds and the shepherds came back to the Great Peak, they found the shelter broken down and all the meat devoured.

"He!"

"He!"

Emboldened by this success the bears harassed the shepherds by day and by night, so that many of them declared, when they went home that autumn, that they wouldn't return there next spring; and a terrible fame of "Him" was borne around through all the Tatra.

But "He" triumphed. In the gleam of the moonlight, somewhere up on the rocky sides of the Naked Peaks, he stood, like unto a black rock himself, and looked down from on high into the empty valleys. He felt himself to be a powerful and invincible thing, like the mountain wind or a thunderbolt, that none can stand against. In the late autumn sunlight he rolled about on the golden, velvet-soft mountain meadows, in the tall, shining grass, looking like a fir-trunk—alone there, the most powerful of all things. Like he was to the silence of a winter night or to the morning frost that turns all things into ice. The empty, silent woods were once more his undivided kingdom. Gloomy, colossal, he bent branches with his paws as he crossed over immense rotten treetrunks, or he swam through the exuberant grass of autumn, his back showing black amid it like a heavily-laden boat on rippling waves. His wanderings were filled with the sweet memory of the defeats he had inflicted, of his victory, of the rout of his enemies. His kingdom, handed down to him by his forefathers, had again become his exclusive possession.

He rushed down, like a rock broken off among the peaks, upon a fierce bison which had wandered up from the valley forests to the neighborhood of Mount Krzyvan. The bison saw him come running down among the great, old firs which grew far apart from one another. It bent its head, with the frightful horns on its forehead, gave a short, throaty bellow, and set its forelegs far apart, fixing its back ones well into the ground. Thus it stood, like a bridge beaten against by the broken ice of spring. But swifter than falls the red fir on Mount Kierz when the wind breaks it, the bear rushed upon him and struck him with his paw at the back of the neck. Blood spurted out. A loud, bleating sound forced itself from the throat of the wild beast, and, like as two avalanches of rock, rushing down from two opposite mountain walls, meet in the ravine and the stones are piled up in walls and the roar of it fills the firmament, so these two, roaring, joined battle. But the mighty, deadly forehead of the bison hit vacancy. The bear slipped aside and for a second time struck the back of his enemy's neck, tearing off a strip of flesh, which fell off the bison's body like a strip of wood torn from a tree by a thunderbolt. The bison's terrible assailant gave blow after blow, avoiding the heavy but swift movements of the bull bison's horns and forehead. At last the latter, fleeing before death, turned its back and, all red with blood and leaving immense clots of it on the moss and branches it brushed against, began to run away in panic despair, and the sound of its hooves was as the sound of hammers striking the earth. But the silent, old forest looked unmoved upon that struggle.

The bear desired the sun after its fight, so it crossed the Nieftzyrka Valley, going through the rocks at the bottom of the Great Peak, and there, under the rock wall, extremely high up, lying among the scattered rocks, on the scorched grass, it warmed itself in the sun, looking down in lonely pride on the broad lands below where man dwelt. . . . And there was no other animal up there, so high. Lower down, herds of chamois, whistling an alarm, fled with frenzied leaps to the inaccessible, black crags, and above were only rock walls that were no menace and a little hawk fluttering its wings in the blue of the atmosphere, watching for the seven-colored, long-proboscised rock-butter-flies.

Winter came and with it the winter sleep. "He" slept in the shelter of a crag, somewhere in the Hlinska Valley; but while he slept folk in the valleys took counsel together concerning him. For the herds and the shepherds were sorry not to be able to return to the grassy, Dark Fir Meadow, and besides the desire for a bloody revenge boiled in their hearts. And when spring came, fifteen men, well armed with bows, knives and hatchets, with shovels in their hands and carrying iron traps furnished with thick chains, set out into the mountains by a path cut in the rocks.

The bear, already awake, saw them, and again he boiled with the desire to rush at them and scatter them through the woods—and again a kind of terror pushed him back into the thicket. Still, he felt that thin bark is no easier broken when one bends a branch to get at the fruit, than each of these men could be crushed. Now . . . now, the desire to have their blood seized him and would have impelled him to rush down upon them—but a mysterious awe restrained him. Oh, if only one of them would approach him—attack him! That man would be torn in bits, would stain the knee-timber with his blood. . . . His most malicious desire, born of a bloodthirsty vengefulness, was to look a man in the face . . . close, close! But he dared not attack—he felt that there was some strange, unknown, incomprehensible strength in man, in spite of the fact that for "his" arms, he was as the supple, frail branch of a raspberry bush.

Again the herds and the shepherds came to the mountain meadow with oxen and sheep. More of them came, they drove up more sheep and cattle and they brought twelve dogs with them. A noise accompanied their march—singing and playing. The mountains were filled with the whistling of pipes, with the buzzing hum of the bagpipes, with the penetrating music of flutes and the far-echoing howl of long trumpets. The men marched thus, as it seemed, to frighten the animals away and to proclaim beforehand their occupation of these upper wilds, their conquest and the establishment of their rule over the Dark Fir Meadow.

Forerunners had already dug, with immeasurable difficulty, deep pits in the rocky soil, had covered these pits with intertwined twigs and branches, which were covered again with moss. This was for the trapping of wolves. For the bears they had set iron traps.

But "He," on the very first day after the oxen were driven up, rushed out of the knee-timber at the point of noon, having set eyes on a great, gray ox. The ox saw the monster before it attacked and bellowed in mortal fear. Raising its tail aloft, it took to its heels. But, in spite of the fierce attack of three dogs which had time to run up, the bear overtook the ox, and it fell under the blows of his invincible paws. A reinforcement of two more dogs and seven herdsmen ran up. "He" retreated from the dying ox into the undergrowth, but he had let men know that he was there, that he reigned, and had replied to their triumphal entry of his kingdom.

He had taken up the challenge, he had shown that he had not weakened.

And on a certain dark, drizzly night he decided to renew his attack, and that in the very center of the camp, on the sheep-pens. But suddenly as he emerged from the knee-timber a terrible pain penetrated him, and the long, pointed, iron teeth of a trap sank into his hind-leg on both sides. He roared with pain and tried to pull his leg away, but the iron teeth did not let go, and a thick chain and an immense log of wood dragged behind him, rustling and clattering. Roaring continuously, he began to fling himself about, dragging the log behind him, but he could neither free himself nor could he retreat. The chain and the log caught in every branch of the undergrowth, in every root of the knee-timber.

The black, drizzling night rolled slowly on above him, above his terrible roaring, above the howling of terrified wolves and the fierce barking of the dogs, which had surrounded afar off the scene of his misfortune. At times a gloomy crag looked out from among the clouds, overhanging the abyss as if curious what was happening down below, where things live, where they are born, where they die.

And dawn came. Pale light flooded the valley, and at once men emerged from the shelters with bows, hatchets and clubs in their hands and cautiously, slowly, with the barking dogs as their vanguard, began to move upwards. And then they stood in amaze, for they saw "Him"; they knew him by his size and his black coat. He was perhaps eight times a man's height above them with the trap, the chain and the log—up among the branches of a mighty fir, which, mad with pain and fury, he had climbed. All about below there were little trees torn up by the roots, crushed and splintered branches, broken in pieces by his claws and teeth, crumpled bushes of knee-timber, rocks, heavy as millstones, torn out of the earth.

The men stood and looked, amazed, not daring to approach.

"He!"

Then one of them bent down, took up a stone, fixed it in his sling and flung it. Immediately a second did the same, and others drew the bows they had with them. A hail of arrows and stones began to fall on the branches, the tree-trunk and the bear. At that he rushed down to throw himself upon the men—rushed down bloody and wounded, with more than one missile sticking in his body. He leapt towards the band of his assailants. The dogs retreated first, whining, and scattered. With them the men retreated—hastily. Only one highlander remained behind. He was tall and broad-shouldered, and held an iron pike which was stuck into a birch-branch. He stood with the handle of the pike resting against a rock and the sharp point forward.

With the trap dragging behind him "He" came leaping towards the man, and when he was a few paces off he stood up on his hind legs to hit his enemy with his fore paw—and his own breast was pierced with the projecting iron point of the pike.

Then he looked at a man face to face, as he had desired. A hatchet, thrown by one of the herds, barked through the air and cut into his skull behind the ears. Immediately afterwards a second hatchet struck him in the neck, a third on one of his fore paws. Stones thrown by hand began to hail down on his body. He fell over on his side with the pike in his breast, breaking down some little trees with the weight of his fall.

The men jumped forward, the dogs ran up to him. . . . Two curs, ripped up by his claws, died with terrible, dull groans. But arrows, hatchets, clubs and stones, coming from nearer and ever nearer, made him lose so much blood that it grew dark before his eyes and his limbs refused him their service. Only he saw approaching, as through a mist, the tall, broad-shouldered highlander who had held the pike before him, and then he felt a terrible blow from a club on his forehead—a blow that shook his whole being and brought his head down to the earth.

Then again he saw men at close quarters, above him. . . .

The Dark Fir Wood was vanquished. "His" monstrous skin, stretched out and fixed to the earth with pegs, was drying in the sun.

[94]

5.

THE WINTER MAIDENS

ACIEK SCYRBULARZ was a highland shepherd all his life until ill-health got hold of him. Something went wrong with him inside. Maybe it was from scrambling up the high peaks, and maybe it was a dispensation of Providence—none could tell. His heart was affected. Willy-nilly he had to stop shepherding, since his weakness prevented him from going up into the Tatras. He had to sit at home and potter round his cottage like an old woman—he who, when he went with his flock to the pastures, in June, did not return until the autumn, did not even come down for the harvest. He had been sitting like that for twenty years already, and he was sixty years old.

And then came a day in the month of May, a day so warm that it was more like a day in July. A lovely, scented breeze was coming from the Tatras. Maciek came out in front of his cottage, looked round and breathed deeply.

"Oh, Lord! Oh, Lord!" he exclaimed.

He began to walk straight before him. He went on and on, because the lovely, scented breeze from the Tatras lured him. A desire to immerse himself in it, as in water, arose in Maciek's heart. One gets into the water when one's muscles are tired and one's whole body weak, and soon one feels better.

So Maciek Scyrbularz went forward, and somehow he was able to walk. He did not feel the terrible pain in his heart which had hindered him from climbing the mountains. . . . How he had cursed and how he had mocked himself! He, a highlander, born in the mountains, he a shepherd of the high peaks, a fine fellow, alert as a shepherd's dog, he who hadn't felt himself climbing—he couldn't go up! He had mocked himself, and cursed, and sometimes wept. Well, not even sometimes, but often did he curse. He would sit down sometimes in a lonely place where he couldn't be seen by anybody, and he would weep just terribly. Up there above, the sheep were moving towards a steep rock, the chamois were skipping over moving stones, a dog was rounding up the sheep, barking at them; and he, first among the shepherds, was sticking at home!

His neighbors teased him a good deal, too. Very few noticed that he was ill. They just called him "gaffer" and scorned him. It's in human nature to scorn the weaker. The blind, the lame and the weak, like the poor, do not evoke pure pity, but a kind of hurtful, pitying scorn.

So it was with Maciek.

He had nobody to complain to . . . to complain to somebody always brings relief. In the first place he had neither wife nor children—and then his dog, Singer, had died of old age long ago. This dog, Singer, who had grazed sheep with him for twelve years, went shepherding with Stas Cudzikowy for another year; but then it couldn't climb, for it began to lose the use of its back legs. So Cudzik brought the dog to Maciek, and it stayed another two years with him, until it was fifteen. It looked up at Maciek, as it lay at his feet, with its dim eyes, and Maciek smoked a pipe, sat on the bench and talked.

Various things he said, and sometimes he cried over the dog.

Folk laughed at it and pitied him, and sometimes they came up on purpose to listen.

"Listen, listen," said they, "Maciek's talking to the dog."

"Wait and see if the dog'll answer him."

But the dog made no answer, only listened, while Maciek went on talking and talking. . . .

"Singer, old boy, do you remember when we were benighted with the sheep on the High Green Rock? Goodness me! Jarka fell down and was killed. We couldn't get down, for the darkness came on so suddenly. . . . Do you remember when the wolf got at you? . . . it was somewhere about Michaelmas, or at the end of October, in the autumn. We had started down, towards home. Wouldn't that wolf have given it to you, if the spikes round your neck hadn't saved you? What a wolf it was! Not often does one come across such. You were never a weak one, were you, Singer lad? . . . Singer, how was it when we were hauling manure on sledges, and an avalanche overtook us? The snow covered the horse and the sledge . . . down it came, all of a sudden, and even the big forest near the top of the mountain couldn't stop it. Lord, how it crashed down! If it weren't for you, Singer, I shouldn't be here today. I'd fainted, and I should certainly have died. But you warmed me and kept waking me; and I pulled myself together, and somehow dragged myself home. I got home without the manure or the sledges or the horse, to be sure—but I was young and I soon got over it.

"Singer, do you remember when Jan Zatrencianski came to steal sheep on our meadows? He was a fellow! You wouldn't find one like him either on this side of the Tatra or on the other. That was a fight! You woke and barked. I ran towards the grazing grounds with my brother Jendrek and Walek Mardula. They came on twice, the same in number as we were. If it hadn't been for you and the other dog, Bystra, we couldn't have beaten them. They were terrible, furious fellows. I still have a hollow place in my head, where they banged me with a piece of rock."

Singer would listen and gaze at Maciek with his dim eyes. . . . So long as the dog lived it wasn't too bad for Maciek, but when he died Maciek had nobody to talk to. Maciek didn't want to talk about the mountains with other highland shepherds, now as old as himself, or with the new, the younger ones. Nay, he even avoided such converse and shut himself up in his cottage. . . . Afterwards men heard cursing and weeping. So obstinate did Maciek become, that he wouldn't even ride up towards the mountains on the horse which he still kept. "If not, then not! If the Almighty doesn't want me to go up into the mountains, I won't go. Maybe I'll go after death!"

But never had there been such a sweet-scented breeze from the Tatra. Maciek just went forward, not even staying to shut the door of his cottage. He entered the forest, which wasn't far from his cottage, and came across a spring, with clear, swiftly-flowing water. Maciek drank from it, and the water was as cold as ice. Something strange happened in him after this drink. It was as if everything turned to ice inside his head. Something bright and clear and glorious filled it. Did the sun get inside his head, or what was it, he wondered.

His heart didn't ache and he went on, though he hadn't been able to climb for twenty years.

Everything became extraordinarily clear to him. Everything round him—every blade of grass, every little branch became quite clear and distinct. "It's as if somebody had put stars into my head instead of eyes," he said to himself.

It was noon when he left the forest behind him. Already he could see enormous slabs of rock, covered with lichen, and firs on the mountain ridge. Higher up was a sort of little meadow, intersected by a torrent. Enormous rocks lay near the torrent. When Maciek touched them he felt that they were hot from the sun. He lay down on a rock with his face towards it, and began to hug and to kiss it. His tears fell in a torrent on the rock, which had lain there since, ages ago, it had been torn down from a peak. Maciek lost himself completely. Twenty years of yearning and grief bound him to that rock.

It had all come back again, again! That twenty years of longing, sickness and bondage had never been. . . . Maciek Scyrbularz had never been called "gaffer," he had never ceased to herd sheep, to climb amid the rocks. . . . He had never sat in his cottage in the village, in the valley, whilst others frolicked with the spring, he had never lamented over himself, he had never wept or complained in his sad, afflicted soul. . . . Singer had never lain at his feet, weak, powerless like himself.

. . . It had all been a terrible, painful, weary dream. . . .

Then he turned his face towards the sky and stretched his arms out wide. . . .

Above him were the immense rocks, white with snow or black where the snow had melted and— the sky, the blue, lovely sky, full of light and of white, light, feathery clouds and mist. . . .

God's own miracle!

Maciek got up from the rock and drank from the mountain spring, and his mind and his sight became yet clearer.

"I see twice as much as before," he thought.

It was a strange sight that he saw, that old fellow!

Andrysh Michna had told him in his youth (Andrysh had been nearly a hundred years old then) of the winter maidens, whom his uncle, Simon Michna Pietrowski, had once seen in the mountains when he had gone up to look if the snow had melted, and whether it was time to drive up the flocks.

Andrysh Michna had been a young boy when his uncle Johym had told him this story. . . .

The winter maidens fly with the wind, with the snowclouds that fly up from that sea which is far away there, and never is free from ice. They are as white as snow, their faces are white, their mouths are white, but their eyes shine like the hoar-frost at dawn, and their hair is all silvered. They have long, white dresses that cling round their bodies like autumn cobweb clings sometimes to the branches of a young fir. When they come down on the Tatra with the clouds (and they generally come on a moonlight night when the moon is full), they at once take hands and begin to dance in a great circle on the mountain meadows, on the rocks, in the valleys and on the frozen lakes, just as they danced on the ice of the sea. He that sees them will not run away. He that looks hard at them will have no good of it. They will charm him so that he will either fall and kill himself or he will go blind; or he will break his leg and never go up into the mountains again. They do not keep in one place, but they fly with the wind over crags and abysses, from valley to valley, sometimes separating into little groups, sometimes sweeping along in a great company. When there are so many of them all together, they dazzle the eyes of him who sees them. They circle right round the Little Pond and the Five Ponds, too. Sometimes it is as if the wind tore one of them out of the ring, and she flies upwards, flutters about in the air, and again comes down and joins the ring.

Thus they frolic about in the mountains until the spring. They sleep when they want to amid

the crags, wherever it is coldest, and they eat the
ice round the waterfalls, on which the sun shines.
Thus the sun prepares their food for them. When
the snows begin to melt, they take to the wind and
fly out towards the sea.

These winter maidens came into being thus, as
very old folk relate: Somewhere in the shadow of
the mountains there was a convent, but nobody
knows now where it was. There were sixty nuns
in it, and a plague killed them all in one day and
in one hour of that day. Now they were very holy.
An angel was flying by, carrying a sack made of
that same webbing as the web that one sees on
grass in autumn at dawn, that weaves itself, for it
is the linen of the angels. The angel was carrying
an orphan's prayer to heaven, and he'd got weary
for the orphan had prayed for a long time. He flew
along, and there he saw sixty white souls waiting
to be carried to heaven by angels—a whole flock
of them, like sheep. "Dear, dear," thought the angel, "how can I let the poor things freeze" (it was
winter). "Wait, I'll take them to heaven." But
what was he to take them in? There were sacks
enough in the convent, but they wouldn't all fit
into one. In the chapel, however, there was a banner of the Holy Virgin, and the angel made haste
to take it. He tied it up as well as he could in haste,
put the souls into it, and threw it over his right

shoulder and flew off. He flew on and on until he came to the Tatra. Then he felt tired with his heavy burden, for there were so many souls and that orphan had cried as she prayed, and her tears were as heavy as lead. It was night, the moon was almost hidden behind the peaks, and the clouds were dark and full of snow. "What shall I do?" said the angel to himself. "I can't pass the night in the mountains, for it's cold and a snowstorm's coming. That wouldn't do. If I fly slowly I freeze to the marrow of my bones, and I'll lose my way in the dim light, for the mountains are big and terrible. If I sit down under a rock, it'll be bitter towards morning; and besides I might fall asleep, and one of the sacks might roll down into the valley. But supposing," said the angel, "I left one behind, it'll be lighter on my shoulder, and I'll fly quickly; and as soon as I get past the mountains, it'll be all right and tight. I'll stow one sack somewhere by a rock and come and fetch it tomorrow. But which shall I leave? Shall I leave the souls of the dead nuns, or the orphan's prayer? If I leave the souls, won't they be disgruntled that I don't take them to heaven at once? If I leave the prayers, maybe the devil, who's always on the lookout, will undo the sack and scatter them like pearls all over the valley—and to gather them up it'll take two days or three. You mayn't lose even one orphan's

prayer, you have to bring them all up to the Lord
God in order, for they're holy things."

He scratched his head, for he didn't know what
to do. But he thought and thought, and at last he
decided thus: As for the souls, a day of eternity
more or less meant nothing at all. But with the orphan's prayers it was another story. If they weren't
brought straight away to the Lord, He would, even
though it was in the middle of the night, go fuss-
ing round finely in the office; for the stars keep
shining behind the clouds, and besides He's old and
doesn't sleep well now. "And if the Lord gets angry with me and won't help me, who will? Those
prayers come from a sorrowful heart, for they're
very heavy. I'll leave the souls. The devil won't
come at them, for Our Lady's banner's about
them."

So he took the banner with the souls from off
his shoulder, and hid it in a crevice under a rock.
Then he rose up high with the other sack, and the
moon still shone a little, and he got up to heaven
by the milky way, flying fast and straight, for he
knew the road well.

But he never thought of the thing that happened.
The devil is always on the lookout. As soon as the
angel had left the banner with the souls and flown
away, he said to the wind—for they're boon com-
panions—"Oh, my dear fellow, couldn't you play

some kind of a trick on the angel? He left those souls in a crevice under the rock, couldn't you let them out? As they're tied up in a holy banner it isn't easy for me to get at them, but you can. Fly along quickly, and let them out for me. I (so he said) have no right to them, but let the angel search for them a little!"

At that the wind flew and blew with all its might. At once the banner came undone and the souls flew out all over the place. They flew one after the other, like doves out of a cote. Far and wide they flew. The wind wondered that there was such a flock of them; but the devil only grinned, struck sparks out of the rocks with his horns, and went off with himself. Down to the earth he went.

The wind marvelled and made off towards the frozen sea, for spring was already on the way and it was a winter wind. But the souls cried after him: Since you were so good as to set us free from that crevice, where we were cramped a bit, we'd rather go with you, so take us with you. We'll dance for you so that you won't weary on the way. It isn't any wonder that they wanted to dance, for they were young girls, though they were nuns, and one can't dance in a convent. There was nothing to pray for, since they were already dead, and what one prays for is a good death. The wind took them, and ran off with them towards the frozen sea.

As soon as dawn came the next day the angel came. He found the banner, but not the souls. "Confound it all, how the devil did you get undone?" said he to the banner. "How am I to find those souls?" He flew about among the peaks. God help him, he found nothing. He scratched his head. He cursed, and he thought: "If they've gone, they've gone—'tis as they wished it. I'll put the banner back where it was, nobody saw me take it yesterday for 'twas dark, and nobody's been out yet today, for it's very early, and nobody will know what happened. I'll hang it up where it was before, and there's an end of it. I won't bother about the souls any more. Let anybody that finds them herd them together, and take them to heaven."

He flew off well pleased, for the souls were heavy and he wasn't used to carrying heavy weights. It's only once in a thousand times that an angel has to carry so many souls, and he'd never been ordered out to a war as yet, for he was a young angel and so had only been on duty round about villages.

So those souls turned into the winter maidens. There, where the winter wind flew, they flew with it. They were terribly homesick on the frozen sea, and so they flew towards the mountains in autumn; but when the spring was at hand they went back again with the wind to the sea, for the wind was their guardian and they didn't want to separate from it. The wind was pleased and they were pleased. The wind played and they danced. But heaven forbid that anybody should look at them. At once they avenged themselves.

It was these winter maidens that Maciek Scyrbularz saw before him.

That was at the Five Polish Lakes, towards the west. Maciek had climbed up on to the bank of the Great Lake, from Roztoka, near the Great Waterfall. The lake was frozen and the winter maidens were dancing on it in a ring.

Maciek was terribly frightened and wanted to retreat, so that they shouldn't see him, for he knew what threatened him. But he was sorry, for it was a sheer marvel to look at. The ice, already thin, became green and red and gold in the sun, and they, too, gleamed red and gold and green by turns. He stood staring.

But they didn't see him, they just danced in a ring.

Then suddenly old mother Nature got the better of Maciek Scyrbularz. He'd been a dancer in his youth, he'd loved it. He'd danced after the girl who partnered him like a cock after a hen, bending from time to time and clapping his hand on the floor. . . . His dancing had been ended when his climbing had come to an end. But how he had loved it! Once he had heard the music his feet danced of themselves. Then afterwards when he heard music a lump would rise in his throat, for he couldn't even dance a few steps.

How he had been used to dance here at the Five Lakes!

His eyes became so clear-sighted that he saw almost every stone on the crags in Woloszyn. His light sandals had danced all over those rocky slopes as he followed the sheep. They had danced to music and without music, to the pipes or without them. He danced at Opalone, he danced at Krzyzne, at Walentowa, under the walls of Liptow, above the Lakes, near Kolo on the Spiglas Ridge. . . . When he whistled as the shepherds do, the whole valley re-echoed to it.

Hundred and two, hundred and three . . .
The shepherd stands 'neath the fir tree,
Sheep of his have strayed away
In the dusk of dying day.

Hey, his old nature got the better of him! Before you could say a word he was within the ring of the winter maidens, and had joined hands with them.

And on the green and golden mirror of the lake, beneath which, as all knew, there was a terrible abyss of water, stood Maciek Scyrbularz, with floating gray hair, and he stamped and whistled, while the winter maidens rushed round and round, like a cloud in a mountain gorge, whirled about by the wind.

Suddenly the wind blew hard and howled. The winter maidens were blown together in confusion, they melted together into a cloud and rose up into the air above the Deserted Valley, going towards Zawrat, towards the north. There was a gleam, it grew white, faded and disappeared as at a spell.

Maciek remained alone on the Great Lake, on the ice.

A terrible, piercing, penetrating pain shot through his heart. Maciek shrank and bent down. So great a weakness came over him that he lay down on the ice.

"Yet once more I've seen the mountains, and once more I have danced. Come quickly now, dear death!"

6.

ZWYRTALA THE FIDDLER

 LD Zwyrtala died and his soul set out to heaven, moustached and with a fiddle under his arm.

He got to the gate and looked: it was shut.

He thought to himself: "Better not bang at the gate; they're asleep."

He sat down on a stump near by . . . sat and sat but pretty soon he wearied of it, took out the fiddle, tightened its pegs with his teeth, strummed on its strings, leant it under his left arm and drew the bow across.

He played softly at first, fearing to wake them, but, warming to his playing, he pressed harder on the bow. Playing there, he called to mind his old woman, who'd stayed behind on the earth and, at the thought, immediately began to sing:

May the bachelor's abode ever blessed be!
Everywhere I look around, there my wife I see. 2

As he sang—and he sang loud—he heard a voice from behind the gate saying::

"Who's that there?"

"Saint Peter!" thought Zwyrtala to himself, but he answered boldly, for in Empress Tessa's time he'd been pressed and had served in the cuirassiers for twelve years over there.

"It's I."

"And who's I?"

"Zwyrtala."

"What're you yelling for?"

"I'm not yelling at all, only singing."

"To the dev—" (the voice broke off) "with such singing. Why ever did you come so late?"

"Right enough, I'm a bit late, but I only died towards evening."

"Towards evening? Then you should be but half way here!"

"Well, Saint Peter, I'm brisk—I'm a highland-man."

"Then where d'you hail from?"

"From the mountains."

"From Novy Targ?"

"Yes."

"And from what village?"

"Oh, if I tell you you'll be none the wiser. You don't know the country over there, do you?"

"I know everything. Where d'you come from?"

"From Mur."

"What's your name?"

"Maciek Galica."

"And your nickname?"

"Zwyrtala."

"And your place?"

"Sentzek."

"Well then, sit there, Sentzek, till daybreak . . .
and don't make a noise."

"All right, I won't. Good night to you, sir."

"There, there! Quiet!"

Maciek Zwyrtala sat there quietly for a while,
but it got a bit cold towards morning, though 'twas
midsummer and again he strummed on the strings.

Lo and behold, a little head—one, two, three
little heads showed over the gate!

They were little angels' heads.

"Ow! Ow!" said one of them. "How nicely he
plays!"

When Zwyrtala heard that he brought his bow
down hard on the strings—on all four at once—
and out came a march:

Oh, the Magyar drinks, the Magyar pays!

"Oh, how beautiful, how lovely!" cried the
little angels. "What sort of a tune is that?"

"That's a bit of robber music."

"A bit of robber music—a bit of robber music,"
the little angels began to repeat, and they clapped
their hands. "Oh, how lovely!"

Suddenly the key grated in the lock and the gate
opened wide; the gatekeeper of heaven, Saint Peter,
appeared in it.

"Zwyrtala!"

"Here I am."

"Come along in."

"No need to ask twice into heaven."

But in a flash the news was all over heaven that a highlandman who played the fiddle had come, and it came to the Lord God's own ears as, having risen early, He sat before His porch, smoking a pipe. He was doing no work, for it was a Sunday.

Zwyrtala hadn't yet been given quarters when an angel came up, but not a little one this time in a little, white shirt and white wings, but a big one, in silver armor with a flaming sword at his side and rainbow wings, and he said:

"Zwyrtala!"

"Here!"

"Is it true that you can play?"

"It's true."

"The robbers' dance?"

"Aye."

"Would you play it?"

"Why not? To whom?"

"To the Lord God Himself!"

Zwyrtala scratched the back of his ear: but only once. He was a Galica and the Galicas were all bold fellows.

"I'll play it."

"Then come along!" said the angel, speaking with a highland accent.

"Would you kindly tell me, sir, if you were ever in the mountains?"

"I was," said the angel.

"But when? Excuse me, sir, for my boldness in asking you."

"When the Poles fought the Tartars in the Koscieliska Valley I was there to help them."

Zwyrtala looked incredulously at the angel. He was young—not more than twenty.

The angel laughed, for he understood Zwyrtala thinking that way.

"We don't get old here, in heaven," said he.

Zwyrtala got ashamed and answered: "Don't wonder, Sir. Could one take in everything in heaven at once? On earth we don't understand everything and how could I here."

"Well, come on!" said the angel, and went in front.

He went along a street—a wide one (Ludzimirska Street in Novy Targ was nothing to it, why, nothing at all!). There were silver houses on both sides of it, where the saints dwelt. Then they came to a golden one, and before it, sitting in the porch, was the Lord God Himself! He was smoking a pipe.

Zwyrtala made his best bow and the Lord God nodded to him.

Round about were angels—small ones, big ones, archangels in golden armor, men and women saints and those others that are in heaven, men and women—heaps of women! They'd run from all sides to hear the music! 'Twas a wonder how they hustled to get in front, those souls!

"Now then!" said the Lord God, "Zwyrtala, play!"

And Zwyrtala bowed himself again before the Lord God and said:

"I most humbly bow to Your Grace, mighty, all-powerful Lord! Does anyone happen to know if there are any young men from Podhale here in heaven?"

"What for?"

"Because one plays better when they dance."

The Lord God laughed and made a sign to the angels. Two of them flew off but came back with nothing.

"There are a few from Podhale, but they're old," reported one.

"That's no use," said Zwyrtala. "How could an old man dance! And where are the young ones? For sometimes young men, too, die!"

Then Saint George said: "You'd have to seek them in purgatory."

"True enough! You say well, young sir. In pur-

gatory! said Zwyrtala. "That's where they'd be—
lots of them!" I know them! Jasiek Mardula, that
Brzenk of Lysintsa killed because of Bronka Hor-
ani, or Franek Macey—they hanged him in Mikulas. Just finely he robbed and set fire to four inns in
Luptov; but maybe he's in hell? Or there was Mayertsik, Peter Mayertsik's son who was killed by
a cart with ore in it in the Skupniov clearing—he
was terribly fond of fighting—oh, if *he* came here!
There wasn't such a dancer in a hundred villages
round."

But the Lord God made a sign with his hand.

"Play!" He said.

"What tune?"

"The robbers' dance."

"Here goes, then, the robbers' dance."

Zwyrtala tightened the pegs with his teeth,
tuned up, drew his bow across the strings and
played it right through, beginning with:

> *Oh, Janitzek, heart of mine,*
> *Where's the feather that was thine—*
> *Given by me?*
>
> *Dearest, when to war I rode,*
> *Fell it where the river flowed*
> *Full and free.*

continuing through:

[121]

Oh, chief of ours, chief of ours,
Good robber-boys hast thou, by all the power!

and so on down to:

For here the robbers dance so gay.

He played everything down to Amen.

The Lord God nodded His head. He liked it. Then the saints and angels followed suit and the saved too; nay, even, I may say, they couldn't praise Zwyrtala's playing enough! And he was most awfully glad and his moustaches bristled.

Well, but listen what happened afterwards. The Lord God went into His dwelling and then the men and women saints and the angels kept saying to Zwyrtala: "Play! Play!"

And Zwyrtala made no reply, but started the Mientushanski tune at once:

When among the meadows I do gaily sing
'Tis as if the organ in the church did ring.

And they all cried out: "Oh, how lovely, oh, how beautiful!"

Thus did Zwyrtala play and sing and what do you think happened!

Saint Joseph, the foster-father of the Lord Jesus, was crossing heaven when he heard a soul singing (some girl's soul it was):

[122]

When I was a little one, only twelve months old,
To me came there singing all the boys so bold.

Saint Joseph listened, and he hadn't heard it out
when, from another side there came a voice that
sounded like a man's:

Maiden if thou wert not of our clan and race
I'd have killed the fellow that looked upon thy face.

And Saint Joseph hadn't heard that well
through, when lo and behold! from yet another
side came an angel's tenor, so loud and strong that
it thundered through heaven:

Strike, oh Lord, that shepherd dallying with a maid,
While his flock, uncared for, through the peaks have
strayed.

Saint Joseph caught his head on both hands!
"My hundred forefathers, whatever's that?" he
said.

He ran towards Saint Peter and there, in the
very place where saved souls are supposed to be
learning angelic hymns, there wasn't archangel
Gabriel standing with his golden baton and his
trumpet, but Zwyrtala, sitting on a chair and fiddling, and round about him men and women souls
and angels sang, already fairly correctly in chorus:

[123]

Homeward lies our way now—dark night's here.
May it not be for us—void of cheer.
'Mid Hungarian nobles—wealth untold,
For our hands since we are—strong and bold.

"Lord Jesus Christ!" cried Saint Joseph and hastened on, faster still, to Saint Peter: "Whatever's up here?"

Just that very moment the archangel Gabriel came up to him and said that nobody in heaven wanted to sing any way except to a highland tune; not even Saint Cecilia!

"Zwyrtala's teaching them," he said. "It's something extraordinary. They were to have learned new hymns—tomorrow's Our Lady's festival—and none of them knows anything."

Night came and found them still listening. From every side highland tunes sounded. All heaven re-echoed with them.

In the morning Saint Peter said to archangel Gabriel: "This can't go on. Couldn't you call up this Zwyrtala, Sir?"

"All right, then!"

Zwyrtala came with his fiddle under his arm.

He bowed.

"Zwyrtala!" said Saint Peter "Would you go away somewhere?"

"Out of this?"

"Yes."

"Away from heaven?"

"Just so."

"But where?"

"Where?" repeated Saint Peter. "Where? That's just what I don't know."

And he fell a-thinking.

"And why should I?" asked Zwyrtala. "Why, they sent me here when I died."

"That's just it."

"I didn't steal or kill or fight."

"I know, I know!"

"Well, then, what?"

"But everyone in heaven's been singing highland songs since you've come."

"Oh, that's it, is it?"

"Zwyrtala!" said Saint Peter (then he paused). "Where can he go from heaven?"

But Zwyrtala kept silent a moment, scratched the back of his ear and then said: "Oh, please Your Grace, don't make your head ache over that! I agree on the spot. I'm off."

"Where to?"

"To where I came from."

"To the earth?"

"Just that."

"And I thought of putting you on some star. . . ."

"I don't want it. You needn't look for any star. I'm off down there."

"Out of heaven?"

"Oh, I'll find heaven there too! I'll go through the woods and the valleys, playing. I'll see to it that the old tunes aren't forgotten. When a boy sits by the sheep with his fiddle I'll play to him softly from behind a crag. When a girl sings by her cows in a mountain meadow, I'll help her. When the old highlandmen go to cut wood in the forest, I'll make sound in their ears the songs their fathers knew."

"And, if none be there, there'll be water in the torrents and frozen lakes, when the wind whistles over the ice. There'll be the forest—I shan't weary there or cry for heaven . . . While I yet lived I often asked the Lord God to let me, after death, stay forever in the mountains. I want no other heaven, I wouldn't change the mountains for seven heavens."

"Well, then Zwyrtala, go! for you'd make us all highlandmen here in heaven. . . . And you won't feel wronged?"

But Zwyrtala raised his fiddle quite up to his head in salute.

"Where my heart is, is heaven," said he.

And he made his best bow and went out at heaven's gate, down the high road towards the earth—it was night. He went down the Milky Way, his fiddle under his arm, and when he felt himself once more in freedom he cried aloud, "Hu! Ha!" and lifted his bow high and struck up:

Come I from the mountains where the torrents leap—
Where the rain has bathed me, wind has rocked to sleep.

Krzywan, Krzywan, Krzywan, why art dreaming so?
Has the white snow clothed thee, doth thy wild wind blow?

Wild goats of the mountains, whither lies your way?
In the Feather Valley, there the wild goats stay.

Janitzek, Janitzek, thunder bears thy name.
Through a hundred valleys echoes loud thy fame.

'Tis no shame, a robber in a mountain race.
A robber sits in heaven, in the foremost place.

And Zwyrtala went forward, down the Milky Way, singing as he went, till he reached the rocky paths in the peaks and on further, into the depths of the Tatra.

7.

OLD WALTSAK'S DAUGHTER

SCARCELY had the first wife of Johym Walcak, that lived behind the water-meadows, closed her eyes, when he began to look round for another; for he wasn't old and had a big, prosperous farm that needed a mistress, and there were two children by his first wife, five-year-old Zosia and eight-year-old Jas.[1] But their stepmother, whom Walcak took from somewhere off Skrzypne way, a young and greedy wench, wanted to get everything for her daughter that she'd had by a farmhand in her own village. So badly did she dispose her husband to his own children that he quite ceased to care for them. He settled his whole property on his wife and her descendants and the only thing she couldn't get from Zosia and Jas was what their mother had left them. But that was a good deal more than they would have had from their father, so that even without an inheritance from him they were extremely rich.

Their stepmother would fain have beaten them often, but once when she caught little Zosia by the pigtail and hit her in the face and Zosia began to cry, Jas caught up a poker from near the stove and hit his stepmother so hard on the arm that it dropped as if dead. She shrieked, seized a milking-pail and rushed at Jas, but he stood his ground

[1] Pron. Yash, equivalent for Jack or Jock.

boldly with the poker in his hand, not retreating a step, and his eyes glittered so fiercely, that she got really frightened.

"If I don't kill him," she thought, "he'll kill me . . . if not now, when he grows up."

She dared not hit him, and then Jas said to her:

"Look here, if you touch Zosia ever again, I'll knock all your teeth out with a bit of rock and I'll take your baby out of the cradle and give it to the pigs to eat."

From that time forward the woman glared wrathfully at the children, abused them, called them names, but she didn't dare to beat them. She hated Zosia more than she did Jas, for Zosia was prettier than either of her daughters, the one that she had by the farm-hand and the other that she had by Walcak.

As Johym's house beyond the water-meadows stood far away from the village, Jas and Zosia were mostly alone together, and they loved each other very greatly. They were scarcely ever seen apart. Jas would have let himself be chopped into bits for Zosia, and Zosia would have thrown herself into the water for Jas, if need were.

They kept on growing, and at last they were grown up. Jas grew into a lad and Zosia later on into a wench. They were wonderfully like each other, good-looking like all the Walcak family, tall and slender, graceful, of haughty mien, with straight legs and small feet, the best of dancers, with comely faces and well-cut features. The girls of the family were the same, with big blue eyes, and rosy lips, like flowers.

Once to the inn where Jas was dancing came Capek of Capkowka, with a strange man, extremely tall, whose hair fell well below his shoulders, whose face was seamed with scars. He had a broad mark made by a hatchet-cut across his right cheek. In a twinkling room was made for him behind the table. Everyone made way; for these two were famous bandits—Isidor Capek of Capkowka, called among the bandits "the Goat," and Maciek Nowobilski, the mayor of Bialka village, whom the bard called rather disparagingly "the Law." By others he was called "the Flint."

These two sat down behind the table and called for vodka. "Law" drank a pint out of a tin mug and turned the mug upside down on the table, but somehow or other nobody else sitting at the table did likewise. Maciek turned aside with a slight gesture of scorn, and his glance fell on Jas Walcak, who was dancing. He was just doing the pandoor's dance and the fiddles were playing the tune:

In the open field,
In the open field,

Is a lime tree growing,
And hard by that lime,
And hard by that lime,
Cold water is flowing.
And he who his thirst,
And he who his thirst
Therein is slaking,
A share of the field,
A share of the field
Will now be taking.

Maciek looked on carelessly, but soon his glance grew keener and dwelt on the lad. With the eye of an expert he followed his movements, looked first at his legs, then at his chest and shoulders, then at his head. He watched, and he moved his head from side to side once or twice, in token of admiration. Now Maciek wasn't the man to do that much, for he knew the world from Buda to Cracow, and hosts of people, among them being fellows who, when they stood up, looked as if they could tear the world into little bits. He himself was in the first rank of these, he had the strength of an ox and the dexterity and lightness of a roe-deer even then, though he was fifty years old. And so when he moved his head from side to side as he watched Jas dancing, it must have been dancing indeed!

He asked Capek, indicating Jas with a movement of his brow:

"Who may that be?"

"Jas, Johym's son, from beyond the water-meadows."

"A fine lad."

"Indeed, there's none better in these parts than he, godfather."

"Tell him to go out behind the inn. Let him note when I knock on the table twice with the pint mug."

Jasiek finished his dance. Capek then approached him and told him what Nowobilski had said. Jasiek's heart beat fast and rejoiced, for though he didn't know that it was "Flint" Nowobilski, yet he honored the name as the name of a powerful man should be honored.

And then he was standing behind the inn, before Nowobilski, red with excitement, though his face was wontedly pale, and he trembled with the beating of his heart. Nowobilski looked him over carefully once more, measured with his eye his tallness, the breadth of his shoulders, and of his chest, the line of his waist, and said:

"Lad, would you go with me?"

"Where?"

"Behind the beech tree."

Lights danced before Jas's eyes. He nearly had to lean against the wall. He'd never expected to have such an honor in his life.

"Would you go with me?"

Jasiek caught "Flint" by his sleeve and kissed it below the elbow.

"I would," he said.

"All right. Capek, look after him. In five days we'll be off. Hatchet, knives, pistols, bag! What you lack, lad, we'll give you. But you come from no barren farm, you must have everything there. Fine clothes like you have on today will serve your turn. . . . Now I'm off to Slodycka's, for Joe Slodycka has invited me very heartily to a feast they're having today. God keep you, Capek! Farewell, lad. But you know, you'll have to pass a test. And keep your mouth shut!"

Jasiek didn't go back to the inn; he sat down on a fallen tree-trunk for he was giddy. Maciek Nowobilski, chief of chiefs, had enlisted him in his band. . . . What a power he must have when he ordered Capek like that! Capek, who was over forty and before whom everyone trembled. . . . Yet the thought of the test made his heart stop beating. . . .

For four days Jasiek did nothing but wrestle with anyone that would wrestle with him. He kept jumping over fences and mountain streams, chasing dogs, cutting off branches as he ran past trees. It looked as if he'd gone mad. "Is he a fool, or what's the matter with him?" asked folk of each other when they saw him running and jumping.

"Maybe he's thinking of being a bandit."

"Oh, he's so well off! Why should a fellow like that go thieving? People might rather come to rob him!"

"Nay, but's he's a strong, healthy lad and his nature might get the better of him."

On the fifth night after that on which he met "Law," Jasiek disappeared and only came back a fortnight later. He had passed the test splendidly.

"He'll rival us all at everything," said the bandits. "Except that he won't be as strong as you, 'Law.' God doesn't give everyone such strength as you have."

So for two years Jasiek went out plundering with the bandits. He was called "Marsh" from the marsh that was behind his father's house. The men liked him greatly, though they treated him rather loftily, for they were all older than he was. Even the youngest, Stasek Mocarny, was already twenty-seven, and all of them had given many proofs of courage, wisdom, cunning and strength, having been for eight years united in a band under Maciek's chieftainship. This band (numbering six, for Nowobilski thought there should not be more) lost one man, Juro Osterwa of Spiz, who was be-

trayed by his mistress, wicked Kaska of Bustryk.
He it was that made that bitter song:

She, my little sweetheart, did not faint away.
When they came to take me she gave the rope that
    day.

and again there was that sad, that tragic song the
robbers were wont to sing:

Forth they lead me faring, what a fate preparing!
They are leading me, dear, to the gallows tree, dear.
I had been another hadst thou chid me, mother;
Had I erst been beaten, idle bread not eaten.
I had been another, hadst thou chid me, mother—
When they hang me high, dear, shame on thee will lie,
    dear.

But again the wenches, taking the part of Kate,
who had been forsaken by him and was afterwards
revengeful, sang:

Had it been with me, boy, as it was with thee, boy,
I had worn an eagle's plume for all the world to see,
    boy.
Well it was for thee, lad, with thy feather flying—
But ill it was for me, lad, with a small babe crying!

It was someone to be Juro's successor that
Maciek Nowobilski had sought for a whole year,
but he couldn't find one till he came on Jas. Not

everyone, however stout and bold, was willing to
go with Maciek; for to go plundering with him
one must have legs of iron, wings on one's shoulders, a back made of steel, hands of brass and a
head of copper with five windows to it. That
meant one must be a tireless marcher, like a wolf;
swift as a deer, strong as a bear: and one's skull
must be hard enough for all emergencies. One
must be able to see not four, but five ways at once,
and be watchful every way.

Zosia was worried about Jasiek, for she was very
pious and, unlike other girls, she loathed the bandit's trade. She wouldn't even look at Michael
Stanik, who loved her and to whom her heart went
out in love, until he gave up being one. He'd never
been a real bandit, anyhow, only just gone out
from time to time with his kinsmen the two Pitons
and Simon of Sikoniowka, and brought away bullocks belonging to the Orawa farmers; but even
that revolted her and she couldn't bear it. But
Jasiek was an out and out bandit and didn't swing
his hatchet in vain, nor in vain see that the locks of
his pistol were in order before he left home.

His father didn't interfere in the matter, and his
stepmother would have been only too well pleased
if Jasiek had never come back, for then she could
have tormented Zosia, making up for past years.
Finally she would have chased her from her home,

and maybe she might have found a way to deprive her of her fortune.

Zosia prayed whole days and nights on end for Jasiek's conversion and for his salvation, and through that she grew ever more pious. But Jasiek never told her where he went. This hurt Zosia greatly, yet her proud heart would never allow her to begin talking to Jasiek about it. And his young soul rejoiced in the fame he won and the admiration and envy with which his fellows regarded him; the adoration and yearning of the girls. The one thorn was that Zosia was grieving over him, and that greatly. But he couldn't change his ways.

And then, one June night, Zosia dreamed that she saw Jas's head, cut off from his body, rolling down over the rocks. It rolled down to her feet, stopped for a moment and looked at her, as if it wanted to say something but couldn't; and then it rolled on over a precipice and was lost in the darkness of the abyss.

This dream, which obviously meant some evil on the way, so terrified Zosia that she decided to speak to Jas.

They were sitting behind the house one Saturday towards evening and looking at the mountains. Green grass was about them, and the alders and aspens, the mountain-ash trees and maples, that grew all around. A little mountain torrent rushed amid the bushes and disappeared into the marsh, and on the meadow blue forget-me-nots bloomed in clumps, and many red and yellow flowers with them. The fields, too, as far as the eye could see, were bright with flowers, and glittered gaily in the sun. The woods had yet their spring color, and further off were the forests, immense, never cut, in which sight was lost, as in a cloud. From the great darkness of these unfathomed forests, circling the horizon, rose towards heaven the Tatra mountains, still thickly powdered with snow. The snow lay late that year. Like immense blocks of gray marble, those mountains stood out. Sometimes pink, sometimes purple or gold light touched their heads and shoulders—already the sun was sinking in the sky, bidding farewell, in radiance, to their slopes.

From the trees came the lovely song of the mountain thrushes, which generally sing best at sunset and at dawn—a song so beautiful that you would say wood spirits with green, transparent wings, hanging on the branches, were chanting the glory of the sun.

Jas and Zosia sat side by side on the threshold and looked towards the mountains. Zosia put her arm round her brother's neck, her other hand she placed on his hands, and said to him:

"Don't go with them any more, Jas, don't go!

You'll lose your head, but, what is worse, you'll lose your song and your salvation. My precious one, my beloved brother, don't go! Do you lack anything? Poverty, God be thanked, comes not near us. The wenches, even without your being a bandit, like you. They follow you themselves, so why should you go with those carousers? And it's a sin! Oh, Jas, it's a sin and an offense to the Lord God. You know what happened to our father's uncle, Jantosh, good fellow as he was? Till now none knows where he laid his head in death. He was lost somewhere, like a stone thrown into the water, and they say that perhaps the Evil One took him, for no good comes of the bandit's merry life! "He's gone with the merry ones" folk used to say, but 'twas with the damned ones he went. For thievery and blood-shedding are wrongs done to men. Oh, Jas, my Jas, go no more with them, go no more! Even now I feel that you might go today or tomorrow. I saw you this morning cleaning your knife and looking to your pistols."

"There," interrupted Jas, "it's just that you don't understand. A girl's a girl. That's one thing —and then, you'd spring behind the birch tree yourself, for you're a lively girl and no mistake, a real Walcak, if it weren't that you're like no other in the world. You're one of us right enough, there's nothing wrong with you; only the heart in you isn't like ours. There's no challenge in you at all. That's why you don't understand, as I said to you."

"Why, Jas, why?"

Jasiek clasped his two hands between his knees and leaned forward.

"Why don't I understand, Jas?"

He was silent a little longer and then he said:

"There, you know, if you only tried it once! If you just once crossed the Tatra into Luptow! What a country it is! There's wine there, and sun, and joy. There's silver there and gold and all sorts of good things for the taking. If you only tried once!"

He began to tell Zosia about the expansive, the wondrous life the robbers led. He told her of the scouting, the reconnoitering to find out where some merchant or rich peasant kept his money, gold ducats, silver thalers or twenty thaler pieces, or oxen or bullocks, or cloth or linen in storeroom or bedroom or cellar or attic in Luptow or Orawa. He told of the approach, of how they stole nearer and nearer—and then how they broke the bars and of those mad leaps into the midst of the room, and the hacking round one with one's hatchet till the others forced the door in—of those terrible, life-and-death struggles.

"Once," he said, "we came to a tavern in Orawa, but we'd chosen a bad day, for we nearly came upon a wedding. We looked—the lights were shining, though it was late at night. 'A hundred devils take them, they're not asleep,' I said to myself. I stole up to the window and then returned to the others and told them what I saw there—a whole crowd and we, as usual, were only six. We had no mind to go back for we had come far, from beyond Kubin even; and yet how were we to get in? I reckoned the inn-keeper and fourteen other men, and a whole lot of women.

"Let's go back," said Nowobilski.

We were all silent and *then* Capek said: "Oh, godfather!" (for he was wont to call him so) "godfather! Who dies of fright the hares will ring his knell. I'm going by myself." Then I said: "I'm going with Capek," and Stashek Mocarny said the same. The Nowobilski laughed and said, said he: "All right! Off with you! I only wanted to test you, but you are, as I see, good boys. Did you ever see me turn back?" And with that he went forward. Capek whistled through his teeth and Nowobilski hummed:

Fix thy wreath on firmly, maid, on thy way to greet me,
And I'll hold as firm my hat, when I go to meet thee.

So we knew we should see something worth seeing. For "Flint" Nowobilski is like this: "if he meets a child on the way he talks to it, takes it up in his arms, kisses it, and don't you dare beat a dog or cat when he's by! When he goes with friends to drink in the inn he doesn't fight, but goes straight home, when he's done drinking. A man of his kind must do so. But when it comes to a fight arms and legs are splintered!"

Stashek Mocarny was to jump through the window when the bars had been torn away, but "Law" said to him: "Don't jump, for there's a crowd of them, let's go straight for the door and in. We'll swing a log and, if the door is shut, we'll drive it in. I know the host has his money in the pantry and nowhere else. We'll go in together."

But Stashek Mocarny said:

"Oh, godfather!" (for we all called him that), "don't wrong me by not letting me jump through the window! I will jump."

"But they'll catch you, for there's a lot of them!"

"Let them!"

"Then go on and jump."

We went boldly up to the window. Nowobilski had a new linen kerchief, wet through. He sent a pistol-shot in at the window to frighten the host and his friends away from it. In a jiffy a pane was broken, he put his kerchief round and twisted it and the bar flew out. The moment it flew out Mocarny was on his two feet in the middle of the room. I went after him without more ado and almost got hit by the back of his hatchet, for he began to swing it round him so that none could approach. Meanwhile our men had found a log, swung it, and bang on the door! They broke it in and rushed into the room.

The host and his company in a fright caught up whatever came to their hands. A battle began. At first it looked as if we were going to get the worst of it, for they were nearly three to one. The women of the company shouted and hit about them terribly so that it was a wonder to see them. They scratched and they bit. But we hit about us too at the men, till they fell like trees in a wood when the woodmen wield their axes. Then we gathered the rabble together and drove it into the cellars—all, that is, that could move, for there were three that couldn't move at all and one not much.

The money was in the store-room under the beams and we took it and whatever else there was and made off; for it was getting light, so long had the fight lasted. We only waited while Nowobilski rushed into the cowshed, sat down by the cow and got milk for the host's children for the morning. We nailed the host by his hair and his sleeves to the door and were off. Capek was whistling between his teeth and Nowobilski hummed to a mournful tune:

[146]

The valley, the valley, the oats are growing there—
To hang thyself than marry ill 'twere better, maiden
  fair.

And Mocarny, with a sack that weighed perhaps a hundredweight on his shoulders, danced the
"little dance" with his feet, while blood streamed
from his head, for someone had given him a
shrewd hack. The blood didn't drip on to the
ground but on to the sack, so it made no difference
to him, for all his care was to leave no tracks behind him. Afterwards Capek poured brandy over
the spot and the bleeding stopped.

"Wouldn't you go with men like that?"

Then Jas went on to tell of feasts with the shepherds on the upper pastures, where whole sheep
were boiled in milk in cauldrons and where vodka
flowed in streams: of dances with the shepherd
wenches and nights of mad love, of those untamed
wildernesses, where for weeks the bandits would
sometimes lie round a fire, amid inaccessible forests, passing the time with songs and stories . . .
while round about them was the free world where
nothing mattered but strength, courage and activ-
ity. . . . "God above, and hatchet or pistol in the
hand. . . . But down there in the valley? Ploughing, mowing, hewing wood in the forest. . . .
Ah."

"God above you, but the devil near you," said Zosia.

"No. Nowobilski says: 'Why should the Lord God work against the bandit? If He'd given everybody equally then nobody would have sought anything from another. The wolf eats the roe-deer, the roe crops the moss, the hunter shoots the wolf. That is God's order. And then, what would the blacksmith do if there were no bandits? He makes the bars and locks. And the music-man? Whom would he play to, and whom would he get money from? And the inn-keeper? One we rob, and the other we drink with. And the mountain wind breaks the trees. There must be stir in the world. If there were no wind and no bandits in the world, it'd come to a standstill.' "

"Oh, it's not so, my Jas, it's not so. Nowobilski doesn't tell the truth. God is angry and the Virgin too. I beg, I implore you by the memory of our dead mother, by all holy things, don't go with the bandits, don't keep company with them. I'd kiss your hands. . . ."

She bent towards Jas's hands, but he drew them gently away.

"Now, what's in your head today?" he asked.

"Oh, I had a dream, a dreadful dream last night. I dreamt that your dear head rolled down from a peak, went past me and down to an abyss."

"Nonsense!"

"No nonsense, Jas, no nonsense! Hell opens beneath you, the devil will get you."

"But with my comrades. Even there they won't desert me. One for all and all for one! That's the bandit law."

"I shall die, Jas, because of what you're doing . . . and 'twould be better if I did."

Big tears began to fall from Zosia's eyes.

"It brings honor. None will call a bandit otherwise than a gallant fellow."

"You've enough of that honor, haven't you? Everyone knows that for two years now you've scarcely been at home, you've been plundering and robbing. The word of you's gone down even to the plains!"

"Wenches like a bandit."

"They'd like you without that. You're rich and comely. . . . Broncia Firkulina told me she'd have you with gratitude any time you wanted, you've only to go to her."

"Oh, if there's not one there'll be another. I've had enough of it. If I mind about anything, it's about you."

"Hey, Jas, you don't love me . . . you don't love me."

"I don't love you? Whom more in the world? You're my only little sister."

"You don't love me, Jas, you don't love me, for you'd give me over to be treated ill."

"What do you mean?"

"If you were to perish, my stepmother'd beat me."

"Beat you?"

"She'd pull out my hair and scratch my face and hunt me from my own home, from my father's house."

"I'd show her! I'd tear her into strips!"

"So long as you were alive . . . but you know, a bandit is here today, and where is he tomorrow? 'Tis your soul that'd suffer and my body. . . . You'll see, neither of us will escape."

Jasiek bent his head.

"That's true," he began after a moment, in a low voice. "Merry but unsure! A fellow's never safe. So many good lads have perished! Within my memory Franek and Woytek Mardula and Symek Tyrala and Maciek Kubiorek and Janko Nowobilski and of Maciek Nowobilski's own band, Osterwa of Spiz and again Franek Budz whom the Orawa peasants bound and beat till they killed him . . . and in our own family there was Jendrek Walcak, called 'the Knot' or 'the Nightmare.' And you should hear Capek when he begins! 'You might pave the bed of the Dunayec river,' he says, 'with the bones of the fine fellows that were hanged at Mikulas, at Novy Targ, in the Orawa castles; or who were shot or broken on the wheel.' That's true!—And if I were to die, then you. . . ."

"I don't matter. It's your salvation that's in peril."

"But your fate is more to me than my salvation. When I think about it it makes me sick. If you were to be hunted forth and to be at people's mercy! If you had to carry water and hew wood! Oh, Zosia, Zosia. . . ."

He sank his head between his hands.

For a long time they sat silent, then Jasiek said: "I swore."

"What kind of an oath was it? To whom?"

"Before a loaded, cocked pistol—I swore faithfulness to my comrades and obedience to the chief."

Zosia clapped her hands.

"Before a pistol! But not before a cross!"

"Yes, but an oath's an oath. It wasn't before a cross that old Stenkala signed away his soul to the devil in return for the devil ploughing, mowing and carting for him for fifteen years, and then he divided the land up between his children and you know what happened. The devil wanted to break the house into pieces, and banged and knocked and shouted down the chimney: 'This is my holding, for I served fifteen years for it, and that faithfully.

The money is yours but the ground is mine. I'll sow sparks and reap flames here! They could scarcely chase him away with holy water."

"Yes, yes, but I know a way. Just wait. We'll go to Ludzimir, to the Miracle-working Mother of God. She'll soon absolve you."

"Absolve me?"

"Absolve you and release you from your oath."

"And you won't be afraid of stepmother any more?"

"No, never! I'm brave everywhere with you!"

Jasiek thought for another minute:

"Let's go, then," he said.

"Oh, my Jasiek!" cried Zosia, and hung round his neck.

Before they started they sat for another moment side by side, their heads together, and twilight fell over the Tatra Mountains.

"When are they to come?"

"Tomorrow."

"Then let's make haste. Tomorrow you'll be theirs no more, but mine and God's. We'll be there by the morning, you'll confess and we'll hear High Mass. Come on!"

Jasiek put his pistols in his belt and took his mountain ax for fear of wolves; for though 'twas summer it was night. But Zosia took her scapular, lest the Evil One should meet them in the wilderness. And so they went forth.

Jasiek couldn't confess, for the priest was ill, and there was even to be no Mass there that Sunday. Then Zosia took Jas by the hand (there was scarcely anyone in the church, only the sexton opened it and went home), led him to the altar, knelt down with him and bidding him fold his hands as if in prayer, folded her own the same way. Thus he repeated after her:

"I, Jasiek Walcak, vow to Thee, Lord God, the Father of the world—To Thee, Lord Jesus—His Son—to Thee, Holy Spirit—and most of all to Thee, Virgin Mary, Mother of God—that I will go plundering no more—and will give up keeping company with bandits—today and forever. And do Thou—Mary, Mother of God—release me from my oath—that I made—before a pistol—to be true to my comrades—and obedient to the chief—and pardon me—my sins—and save my soul—forever and ever—Amen."

Zosia prayed fervently. Jasiek prayed too, as well as he could. He gave a ducat, she a thaler to the sexton and they went away.

They said nothing on the way back and ate nothing, though they walked much more than seven leagues there and seven leagues back, over mountains and valleys. Zosia was praying and Jasiek walked beside her with his head bent.

At last she said to him:

"Are you sorry?"

"My heart's nearly breaking."

"The greater the merit before God."

After a moment Jas said, with tears in his voice:

"My life's no use to me now. It's worth nothing."

"You'll see it will be. Now only 'twill be worthy of the Lord Jesus' favor."

They reached home. They drank some milk, ate an oat-cake that Zosia had on the shelf, and, as they were tired and hadn't slept, they lay down on the bedding and went to sleep in one room. Though it was still day and the sun was high, they went to sleep and slept until the evening.

In the evening Zosia awoke. It was dark. Black clouds covered the sky. It was pitch dark. Jasiek was asleep.

Zosia knelt on her bedding to thank once more the Mother of God for Jas's conversion. Suddenly there was a knocking on the window-pane.

She quivered.

A second time the knocking came—louder.

"Marsh, are you alive there, are you asleep?"

Jasiek awoke.

"What?"

"Are you alive?"—asked the same voice.

"Nowobilski! Law. They've come for me."

"Then let them go," said Zosia quietly, "you're their's no more. Don't say a word."

"Marsh! Aren't you at home? If you are, get up!"

The voice was so powerful and imperative that Zosia heard Jas jump right out of bed.

"Jas!" she cried.

But Jasiek had sprung to the window.

"Is it you?" he asked.

"Of course it is," came the impatient answer. "Didn't you expect us? Why, you knew we were coming. Are you ready?"

Jasiek wavered for a moment. The blood went to his head. He was dressed, for he'd lain down in his clothes. He jumped to the corner of the room where he had prepared his hatchet, knife, pistols and belt, with all its accouterments, powder, bullets, as bandits are wont to have them. He caught up his bag, his hat and his cape from a peg and rushed out of the door.

"Jas!" groaned Zosia, running after him. But he shouted to his comrades "Run away!"

They, not asking why he said it, began to run like startled wild boars.

"What's the matter?" asked Nowobilski of Jas. "Who was chasing you."

"My sister."

"Sister? What kind of a sister? What's the jest?"

"I'm not jesting at all. I'll tell you afterwards."

But Zosia wasn't chasing Jasiek. She fell with

her arms stretched out before her across the threshold of the house and there she lay a long time, so
that they were near Koscieliska Valley before she
came to herself.

She dragged herself back into the house, fell on
her knees by the bedside and began to weep
quietly and to sob.

The whole night till the morning and the whole
day after she stayed there kneeling by her bedside.
She was offering her life to the Holy Virgin, her
youth and her love to Michael Stanik of the Clearing, and her fortune and her health and everything
if only She would have mercy on Jas, would con-
vert him and forgive him for breaking his oath.

Evening came, then night, and suddenly there
appeared to Zosia the figure of Jas, with torn
clothes, pale and bloody, beckoning towards her
dumbly, as if he couldn't speak. Zosia cried: "All
good spirits praise God!" and jumped up, signing
herself with the sign of the Holy Cross, but the
figure moved towards the door and then beckoned.

"Jas, is it you? Jas, brother, dearest brother!"

For the third time the phantom beckoned and
disappeared through the door.

"Jas, where are you going? Why do you say no
word?" cried Zosia, rushing out-of-doors after
him.

She followed her brother through the fields into

the forest—further and further, calling out from time to time: "Jas! Brother mine!"

The woodland she knew ended and the fathomless forest began. She walked in the darkness, and the phantom led her through the thicket, across rotten trunks of immemorial trees, through briars and hawthorn bushes. It led her through herds of flitting does and forest martens. Scarcely, scarcely had the damp, white dawn begun to show itself when the phantom led her to a sloping clearing among the limestone rocks.

There Zosia stretched out her arms and, with a frozen scream on her lips, stood on the threshold of the clearing, among the trees. On the clearing, on the growing grass, lay Jas's corpse. In his hands he held his mountain ax. He lay alone, quite alone. His hat had rolled lower down the slope."

"Jas!"

Zosia rushed towards him and raised his heavy, cold head. His eyes were half open and glazed. In his chest was a little hole and below it were three streamlets of blood.

It was all set down in the song:

They have killed Jasicek on the meadow land.
Why did he not fight them, his axe was in his hand?
They have killed Jasicek on the slope today.
See, his hat has fallen from his head away.

They have killed Jasicek where the grey crags rise,
Blood in three streams flowing from him as he lies.

Zosia threw herself down upon the body and began to kiss it, eyes, face and breast. It seemed to her as if a groaning came out of the earth and she understood that it was the spirit of Jas in torment and cried:

"Miracle-working Mother of God of Ludzimir, I'll give you everything I have if only you save my brother's soul!" And from her breast, yea, from her very heart, there flew forth three white doves: Faith, Hope and Love.

Those three white doves that dwell in every young heart!

Huntsmen from Orawa passing by found them both—a dead lad and over him a beautiful girl, who said nothing and seemed not to hear. They looked at Jas's pistols and saw they'd not been shot off. He hadn't died by his own hand. They said a brief prayer, took away the weapons and buried the body near a rock, making a heap of stones above the place. They signified to the girl that she was to stay there till they came back in the evening, but when they returned they didn't find her there on the clearing. There was a mound of stones and on it they found woodland flowers.

8.

THE SAVAGE SHEPHERD

THERE was a shepherd from Jurgow, terribly savage; his name was Bronislaw Luptowski—called the charcoal-burner, for his face was as black as if he burnt charcoal in the forest, only his great, blue eyes shone under their lashes. It was said of him that when he looked at anyone, even the boldest fellow couldn't keep looking at him and retreated. The shepherds' dogs, in height up to a man's middle, which would leap at a wolf alone, and even at a bear if there were three or four together near a mountain shed, before this Luptowski, when he came to a strange clearing, crouched down and growled from afar. He was so strong, too, that he could break two horseshoes at once like aspen rods. When they shut him up in the prison of Nowy Targ—he happened to have on him Orawa sandals, with heels—he amused himself by jumping on to the stove, which was low there, and from the stove on to the floor, and each time he drove his heels right into the floor, and he made such holes in that prison that all the warders, commissioners and judges gathered together and wondered, and the chief judge of all couldn't help giving him money for that trick, though he did damage; he marked the floor all over wonderfully!

And he was so cross that for nothing at all he hit a person in the face or kicked him, and then before they could look round them, they saw the world upside down. And when he got into that kind of a rage, he ran away from everything and lost himself somewhere in the woods, so that none either saw or heard of him. What he did, no man knew. Did he go robbing, or did he only wander? No man could tell. If he went robbing, it was by himself, for he had no comrades. But he was strong enough to be a whole band of robbers in one person.

"Hey, if Janosik was still alive," he would say sometimes, "we would have a try with each other, which of us would be chief. For with you, you weaklings, what can I do? I could only use you as flails, to thresh with in a barn."

But he only talked like that; for everyone knew that there was no fellow stronger than Janosik and that he carried rocks on his back, and when he jumped he hewed off the top of one fir with his mountain axe, and shot off the top of a second with his pistol, which this shepherd couldn't have done. But that he would have been a good comrade for Janosik, is sure.

And in the winter he worked with his parents at home, for he was very hard-working; in the summer he kept sheep in the mountains, in the Maple Orchards. And though he sometimes left the sheep and wandered somewhere in the Tatra

Mountains, the Ustup chief shepherd was always glad to see him, for he was a real shepherd, when he wanted to be, one that you might look far through the world for. The sheep grazed with him as if they were pigs.

Bears, too, had no great reason to steal up to him out of the wide Jaworzyna knee-timber, for he was as watchful as a dog and had already killed two bears himself. Not with his musket or by means of a trap, God forbid; one of them he stunned with a stone and choked with his hands; the other he pierced with an iron fork.

There were no more such strong men as he was, after him.

Folk would have liked him, for he was a splendid fellow, comely and graceful, and he could talk agreeably and sensibly, but he had one failing, that he was terribly violent and that sometimes he ran amok. Hence folk kept out of his way and called him "the savage shepherd." He had already killed three people in fights, but in those times nobody minded that much.

The girls, too, feared him and ran away from him, but when he caught one of them by the hand, she was his.

And they told of him that with his eyes he so paralyzed the girls that they were afraid to move —just the way a serpent does with birds, so folk

say. And so he had as many sweethearts as he
wanted, for nobody was very keen to come between him and them. He said of himself: "I have
as many sweethearts as there are cones on a fir tree;
but if you ask whether one of them loves me, I
say no!"

He didn't love them, either. Today he was with
one and tomorrow with another, again he would
return and again would find a new one. He had
whatever he wanted.

And what do you think happened? That shepherd fell in love with a wench that grazed cows
near Muran Mountain. Nobody could understand
what happened to him. But he changed so that it
was as if someone had taken his spirit out and put
in another. Where before his eyes would have shot
sparks and his teeth would have gleamed between
his lips, now he only smiled, turned away or went
on further. He drove his sheep towards Muran;
and though he grazed on other folk's pastures, nobody made any objection, for nobody knew
whether that smiling had ended or not, or if it
would quickly cease. He grazed where he would.
He drove his sheep to Muran and said to the shepherds there:

"Go and graze your sheep in the wide Jaworzyna Valley."

"But we're afraid of your chief shepherd."

But he smiled.

"Oh, I've asked him not to hinder you."

Then they went boldly, for they knew that no official paper was worth as much as that request.

And so there was no wrong or disagreement.

And she, that girl, came from the Zdziar region, where there are women famous for their beauty. Her name was Agnes Hawranóowna, and none would have believed that she could so look upon that Bronislaw Luptowski as if he were a tree-trunk. He couldn't manage her at all.

"Little Agnes," he said to her, "won't you like me?"

And says she to him:

"No!"

"Why?"

"Because I don't like the look of you."

And he talked to her as to a saint's picture, and she to him as to a dog. And what use to him were his strength and might?

Another he would have seized by the hand, so as to leave red marks on her wrist, and there would be an end of it! But with this one he only looked up as though to heaven; and seldom does a mother speak as nicely to her child as he spoke to that Agnes; and when the folk saw that he had softened so much, if they had not been afraid because of what they remembered, and it it hadn't been that they didn't know how long it would last, one and another would have paid him back with their fist between his eyes for what had been.

The wench was terribly bold with him. Not only would she not let him into the shed in the evening, but she wouldn't let him into the hut in the daytime, even though folk were there, and if he got in when she wasn't there, she hunted him out afterwards into the fields.

"What do you want here? You're not one of ours, go to your own! What business have you among us? Get away! You devil!"

And he said nothing, only looked at her as if he were saying his prayers, stood up and went away. People said: "It serves him right," but one girl and another were so sorry for him, that they would have been glad to comfort him. But he had no eyes for anyone now but for that Agnes Hawranóowna from Zdziar.

And so it happened that they met one evening among the rocks near the Muran Mountain, she lower down with her cows and he higher up with his sheep. He came towards her and asked:

"Will you let me sit by you?"

"Sit, but so that I don't see you."

"Then you can't bear me at all?"

"I can't."

"But why? There must be some reason for it!"

"There is."

"What reason?"

"Because I've promised Jendrek Hawraniec that's serving in the cuirassiers."

At that, how he jumped up and shouted:

"Then it's only for that! Hey, and I thought it was goodness knows what."

He caught her up in his arms as he would a lamb, and bore her towards the sheep among the crags. She, whether it was because she got dumb with fright, or whether it was because she was so obstinate, didn't even cry out. It was no use crying out, either, for who would have followed him there? . . .

He carried her to a flat place where the sheep were grazing. He laid her on the ground, knelt down by her, and said he:

"You're mine."

"I'm not yours!"

"Then I'll throw you from this crag down the precipice!"

"You won't!"

"No? And who will defend you?"

"You yourself!"

"I myself?"

"Your love."

And it was only then that something happened that never and never had been seen by folk in the world. He let her go; then he jumped and caught the nearest sheep, he threw it down the precipice, he ran about the grass, and threw down the fifty or more sheep he was shepherding, all in a heap, as it were, from the height of two storeys. There was a very rampart of those killed sheep. He was so furious.

Meanwhile she had jumped up from the ground and run to the shed.

When he had finished with those sheep, he must have weakened, for he lay down on his back; night was coming on and he was still visible, black on the moonlit grass. Folk didn't know what he was doing, whether he had fainted or what, but they were afraid to go and look at him.

Still there was no sign of him till the morning, and he never more came back to Muran.

At first they thought, both at the Maple Orchards and there, that perhaps he had enlisted in the army; for just then there came to Lewocha Austrian Imperial recruiting sergeants, enlisting men. But it was not so.

In the night he got heavily up from where he lay and stole towards Agnes' shed, which stood on the edge, under a hill; the dogs didn't bark, for they knew him well. He dragged a stone from the hill with his hands, a stone that scarcely three fellows could have lifted, raised it up above his head

—he knew on which side Agnes was sleeping. Here, here, he would have crushed the roof in and killed her.

He aimed once, then let his hands fall; he aimed a second time—the same; at the third time he flung the stone into the pond, and only said to himself softly: "Oh, little Agnes, little Agnes!" . . .

Such a lad! And he could have demolished all the sheds and all the shepherds in them!

And, as if he was afraid of himself, he jumped into the forest, from the forest into the knee-timber, in among the crags, he ran across the Maple Ridge, let himself down into that old forest that then grew under the Rowienka Mountain. There the red firs were as thick as pillars in a church, and under their branches there was scarce any light. To higher than a man's knee grew ferns, all kinds of plants, sorrel, charlocks, and grass. There was a terribly thick undergrowth. Trees grew thick on the remains of rotten trees, the feet sank into rotten wood. Piled up between rocks, one on another, were trunks, beams, blocks, and everywhere was damp, green moss; and moss hung from the branches, grayish green, long as beards. And among the trees grew tall, yellow flowers—and they would shine sometimes in such a way through the branches that you would have said something evil was looking at you, till you shivered. And when there was no wind, it was so quiet there that there wasn't a stir. Even the water flowing in the torrent down below wasn't to be heard. A forest still as a dead man.

There he stopped, that Luptowski shepherd, and it was still deep night; for he could walk quickly, he could!

He found himself in that forest, and said he: "Hey, forest, forest! either I or you!"

Whatever was it that came into his head? He went clean mad!

He caught one trunk—pulled it towards him— a crash! It crumbled. He caught another, and a third; he broke and tore young red firs, pulled them up by the roots. He jumped at old fir trees with his teeth bared, he tore the bark from the trees, till blood and foam squirted from his lips. Through the wood spread a din, a crashing, a cracking, so that the huntsmen, and the chamois hunters from Zakopane, who were camping for the night not far off, thought that a bear had been caught in an iron trap somewhere near the Frog Ridge (for the Bialka folk were accustomed to lay traps there), and had dragged it towards Rowi- enka. And a bear in a trap breaks the forest most terribly. But it was night, so they were afraid to go there.

Towards morning the noise ceased.

"The poor thing has tired itself out," said the huntsmen. "We must go that way and see if we can't somehow set it free, for it must be tired of being in that trap. . . ."

They went along, then they stopped, as if someone had thrown sulphur in their eyes; even their muskets shook in their hands, and Tyrala's even dropped.

There were great, crushed branches; little trees; broken trees, one on another, so that in the wood there was now a clearing one could see out of; there under a fir-tree was a man in a torn shepherd's shirt, with a tattered belt. He was all bloody, his hair stuck together with blood, he was scratched, with holes all over his body, as if someone had dragged him over a harrow. They got so terrified that they hesitated for a long time, whether to go up to him or to flee.

"A devil went mad, and that's all," said Capek.

"Or he struggled with some spirit and overcame him," said Tylka.

"Oh," said Tyrala from Kościeliska Valley (for he was prone to believe in such things), "I know. Isn't that he who bore his sins like living flesh on his shoulders and tore them with his teeth?"

"Or something has beaten somebody," said Capek.

[171]

"For who knows if a devil didn't perhaps choke the man and throw him there?" said Tylka.

"Eh," said Tyrala, "why should he have danced about the wood with him till the morning? Do you think it's like in an inn, when two fellows get each other by the heads? An evil spirit need do nothing but touch a man! If he touches you with his finger, it's all over with you!"

But old Jendru Siecka, a wise fellow, said nothing, only looked, and then he said:

"What fool's tales you're telling! Nonsense! It seems to me, I must know this man from somewhere. Wait a little! The sun has just shone out clear. Let's look at him."

He approached, he looked, he shouted:

"Why, it's the wild shepherd from Jurgow! Why, I've seen him time after time. He wasn't like that. He must have gone mad, and none made all that confusion but he alone. He's made fine holes in his chest, neck, face and arms with the branches. He's like a sieve! But what has happened to him? Look at him, all of you!"

"But he was a fine fellow, he was," said Tyrala, for now they had all plucked up their courage to come near to him, after Siecka.

"The wild shepherd? Luptowski? I knew him," said Tylka. "If you fell into his hand, you'd soon have chased your heels with your teeth in the air!

I saw how, at a fair at Lewocha, he carried a horse in his arms like a sack of spring grain."

"Hey, I met him, too, time and again," said Siecka. "Once for a joke he stopped the mill wheel at Szaflary with his arms. We were just coming back from town when he did it. The miller ran—what the devil had happened? He crossed himself, so he did. And that rascal held on and laughed. 'What'll you give me?' says he, 'if I let go.' He had to give him two twenty-crown pieces, but he wasn't a poor man, that Kamiński in Szaflary."

"Dad Siecka!" said Tylka, "I think he's still alive. He is quivering."

Siecka bent down and then he, that shepherd, opened his eyes and he whispered:

"Hey, what has got the better of me? These two: A wench and the forest." . . .

And then he died.

9.

KRYSTKA

WAS on an afternoon in late September that Krystka met her Jas.[1]

The sun shone, cold and clear, over the distant meadows; on the peaks of the Tatra the icy hoar-frost had bloomed, and a hard gleam, like that which comes in winter from windows in the church, shone from them. Over the woods hung a luminous mist that quivered, as if church bells had been ringing near at hand.

In the fields lay the oats, laid in rows, golden-like.

A clear-cut, dark shadow fell from the young, scattered fir-trees, but the shade from the elders and the birches was elusive and flecked with light. Where there was a fence, the uppermost rail in places shone like polished steel. Somewhere far off a cart with grain seemed to swim along in its own shadow. Where there was a streamlet the water shone like living diamonds.

The birds flew past silently.

Where the grain had been cut, on the yellow stubble, cattle were grazing. Each cow trailed its phantom behind it, or stood suddenly still in the sun as though made of brass. At times a cow would moo, at times a calf would low. Here and there a shepherd or shepherdess would break into song. On the edge of the wood some children were light-

[1] Pron. Yash, equivalent for Jack or Jock.

ing a fire, the smoke went straight upwards, chased from below by the brilliant red of the flame.

Mountain streams flowed down through the brushwood, with their monotonous, eternal voices.

There was a glassy stillness in the air, and the sun gleamed more brightly than usual on the ice-coated, frozen Tatra; brilliantly it shone, shedding its light expansively over the world.

Krystka was sixteen years old, and was herding cows.

She lay on a grassy hillock near the edge of a field, amid the oat stubble, wrapped in a striped shawl, yellow and green, holding in her hand a whip which she waved above her head. She lay on her back, and her legs, under her tucked-up skirt, were visible to the knee.

She had a strange feeling about her heart, as if something were tickling her under her arms and would fain burst from her breast. Time after time she rubbed her back against the grass, moved, tried to lie more comfortably. Something within her was pulling at her, was making her turn over and over so that now her back, now her face was uppermost.

Then suddenly she burst out singing:

When at length a maiden her fifteenth year has passed
'Tis in vain to guard her, she'll find her boy at last.

And then something rustled above her head and a penetrating man's voice said: "Why are you singing like that, my girl?"

But Krystka did not answer, for there was a dazzling before her eyes. A man stood above her, a young lad that looked as if he had come straight down from the sun. There was metal on his breast that shone, the buckles of his belt shone, the mountain axe in his hand shone, the white jacket over his shoulders, the red stripes on his trousers shone, too, and so did his bronzed face, with its blue eyes, like gentians with the dew on them. Krystka gazed her fill at him, and he saw it and smiled.

"Why do you stare at me like that, eh?" he asked.

Krystka was naturally a smart girl. She roused herself out of her fascination.

"Because you frightened me," she answered.

Again he smiled.

"Am I so ugly as all that?" he asked.

"No, but you rustled above my head and just frightened me out of my wits."

The lad stood there for a moment; obviously he rather liked the look of Krystka. He looked at her sharply, straight into her eyes.

"Are you going a long way?"

"Oh, long enough . . ." and then he added, "up to the Ponds. There are sheep there still."

"What a fine feather you have!" said Krystka, for he bent down just then and the shadow of the feather fell on the stubble.

"It's an eagle's feather. Would you like it?"

"What should I do with it—fasten it to my shawl?"

"Put it here," and he clasped her round the breasts.

"Sit down."

She pushed him away with her elbow, so that his arm flew back, but a shiver passed through her whole body, more particularly down her back.

"Are you a nun?"

He showed a bold face, but he was taken aback. Krystka began to feel quite at her ease. She wanted to say something cutting, but when she looked at his sunburnt face under the dark brim of his hat in which the eagle's feather flared long and slender in the wind, no sharp word would pass her lips. He saw that and smiled yet again.

"Would a man ever think you were so cross?" he said.

He sat down beside her on the hillock.

"I've time to spare," said he.

"Yes, it's early," answered Krystka.

"What were you singing when I was coming here?"

Krystka wondered at herself, for she felt

ashamed, which she had never done before.

"You heard it, didn't you?"

"What was it?"

"I have forgotten."

"Have you indeed?"

"Why shouldn't I?"—Krystka blushed and looked at him sideways.

"Because—," and the lad put his arm round her waist over the striped shawl, and drew her to him.

"Where d'you come from?" asked Krystka after a minute.

"From Gron."

"Then what are you doing by the Ponds with the sheep? Those are the Zakopane meadows, not yours."

Suspicion crept into her mind.

"Oh, I only just said that. I have no sheep up there," he answered.

"Then what brings you here?"

"Oh, I just came, past Lilowa."

"Whither would you go?"

"Up into the mountains. I've to meet someone there."

His eyes shone cunningly and fiercely.

Krystka looked hard at him. He had two knives stuck in his belt, and a pistol.

"Well, well," thought she, "so he's a robber!"

At once she was full of admiration and delight.

"When will you come back?" she asked.

"Perhaps a week, perhaps five days. Will you be grazing cattle here?"

"Yes."

"And what's your name?"

"Krystka. And yours?"

"Jan. Will you kiss me?"

Krystka blushed crimson and bent her head, then she smiled and looked up from under her lashes.

"Will you kiss me?"

Softly she whispered: "I will."

So Jasiek put his arm round her waist and kissed her, and a great delight came to her.

When he went from her up towards the wood near the mountain, tall, white in his white coat, with the long eagle's feather floating in the wind, her heart was full to bursting and she sang out loud:

> *Lad of mine, lad of mine, must you go away?*
> *I'll never cease to mourn it to my latest day.*

From the wood his answer floated back:

> *Though I go a-robbing maiden don't repine.*
> *Send a prayer to Heaven, I shall yet be thine.*

For a long time yet his singing came from the wood, ever more distant, ever fainter, till it began to become inaudible, to melt into the silence of the twilight of the trees. And so he went from her up into the ancient, hoary Tatra, into the frost and the wilderness, into the terrible solitude of the autumn woods; he went singing, merry, with his sunburnt face, dressed as for a feast, glittering with brass and with weapons.

Round Krystka the silence fell.

One sultry afternoon in June Krystka was walking through the fir wood near Woloszyn by the mountain meadow. Far off the metal sheep-bells jingled.

As Krystka went she sang:

Lily wreath, lily wreath, thou hast fall'n from me.
Down the stream thou floatest but I'll not follow thee.

"I'm not a bit sorry," she thought in her heart, and went on singing:

Shepherds, shepherds of the peaks, if the Lord ye fear
Find the wreath that I have lost, bring it to me here.

"If you dare, you damned fools!" she said under her breath.

I have kept it secret but I will no more.
You'll prepare the cradle, I'll make garments four.
You'll prepare the cradle, made of fir-wood fine,
I the tiny garments for him that's mine and thine.

[183]

"Oh, there, what am I singing that for? It's not as bad as all that," she laughed.

She listened for a moment—from afar off the sheep-bells tinkled, few and faintly. She sang on with love in her voice:

I will peck your eyes out Jasiek lad, beware
If you come empty-handed, to work I do not care.

"Oh, I shan't have to do that. There's plenty of silver in the towns of Orava, in the shops of Luptov."

Where's that feather, lad of mine—fain I'd see it wave.
For some maiden's golden lock your floating plume
   you gave.

"Did he, indeed? It floated and fluttered when we met on the pasture that first time. . . . Three years ago come autumn."

Love me, love me, lad of mine—love me still today.
Let no other maiden's glance charm your eyes away.

"If it did! A hundred devils should eat her! She should die on the spot."

She stamped her foot and crooned on, sweet and great yearning in her voice:

Come, oh come, in daylight or come in dreams to me!
Ne'er, awake or dreaming, I cease to think of thee.

[184]

"Where can he be! Holy Virgin, Mother Mary! Where can he be? He was to have come to the milking sheds today!"

Though I have nothing I sing all the day
Like the birds of the air in the forest in May.

"Jas! Jas!" cried Krystka and with outstretched arms she ran towards a high rock near the mountain. He took up the song:

I'm as free, I'm as free as the birds in the sky—
Like a fish in the water—so free, maid am I!
Uha!

If you knew, my maiden, if you could divine,
You'd shut me up in prison for this song of mine.

Gay, proud and gallant to look upon he emerged from the fir wood, white from head to feet—shining!

"Oh, my Jasiek," whispered Krystka, breathless with rapture, and she threw her arms about his neck. "My dearest! My darling!"

"How are you?" said Jasiek. "I'm hungry. Is there any cheese in the shed? Have you any dumplings?"

It was an August evening, fine, moonless, starlit. The wood by Woloszyn rocked lithely, monoto-

nously, in the wind; the firs rustled on the mountain slopes as if charmed into rhythm.

If you looked up you saw stars on them, on the
branches, like golden moths drawn by enchant-
ment to that wood from some golden world. If
you looked higher you saw stars on the crags, as
if the mountains, enchanted, had burst into a flowering of gems.

Krystka was walking through the wood and
wringing her hands. Tears poured from her eyes
and her tangled hair fell on to her shoulders. So
she went, despairing.

When her heart was like to break with pain,
singing burst from her as the waters burst through
a dyke in flood time:

Oh, my heart is weeping, my heart will break with
pain,
Since for my Janicek I wait and wait in vain.
Oh my heart is weeping, soon twill cease to beat
False Janicek treads it neath his careless feet.

Her singing echoed far and wide. Krystka did
not know whence these strange words came to her.
She sat down on a rock and covered her face with
her hands and began to cry. And then again, when
it seemed that her heart would burst, the singing
began again:

Narrow, narrow, narrow tonight my bed shall be
For I know Janicek will not sleep with me.
On the hay that makes my bed, tears will fall like dew,
For the joy that I have lost time will ne'er renew.
Happiness that once was mine time hath borne away,
Gladly, gladly would I die before the break of day.

Her song echoed through the wood. Krystka arose and followed the echo. Hatred and anger possessed her heart. Her song became a howl that echoed far and wide:

If I knew, if I knew what has caused my pain
I would cry to God above nor would my cry be vain.
I would pray that some dark night demons thee should
*   slay,*
That thy body from the field crows should bear away.
Had I known, had I known thou wouldst me betray,
On thy traitor neck a rope had hung before today,

Echo groaned through the wood and Krystka went on with her wild epic:

Wait, oh wait Yadviga, be thou e'er so fair
One night I will meet thee close beside thy lair.
I will look upon them, those grey eyes of thine,
Wait, oh wait Yadviga, vengeance will be mine!
Wait oh wait Yadviga, with thine eyes of grey,
Blood will drain from thee, lass, in the woods that day.

[187]

Blood from thee will drain, lass, blood from thee will
*   flow,*
Dressed in white they'll lay thee in thy coffin low.

She clenched her fists and rushed on through the wood. Wet ferns beat against her feet, brushwood and heather crunched under her feet.

Echo carried her song afar, and the old shepherd Michael Zvijac in Yavorzyna could not sleep. He lifted his head from his pillow and wondered within himself: "What devils are raging through the wood? Have they got bored in hell, or what?"

Meanwhile Krystka went back to the shed near Woloszyn. There was a tumult in her heart, sorrow and a terrible desire for vengeance. She did not walk, she ran through the wood from Yavorzyna, which she had reached unknowing. With her shoulders and her breast she bent the branches of fir-trees, and the undergrowth in her way her hips pushed aside. From time to time she would lap up water from a mountain streamlet. A stag, startled, ran with beating hoofs through a thicket. Krystka, her teeth biting into her lower lip, rushed through the wood towards the mountain pastures. Light shone from the windows and doors of the sheds, which were hidden in the dark shadow of the great tree-trunks and the mighty branches that swept the earth. Dogs barked and ran towards Krystka, wagging their tails in greeting. She kicked the nearest so that he yelped and rushed on towards the shed where, as she saw by the light that shone through the chinks, a fire had been lit.

"Is anyone in there?" she shouted.

"I am," replied Jasiek from inside.

She came and stood in the doorway? In the low, dark room, lit up brilliantly from the side by the fire, came smoke and the thick, stifling smell of the resinous, burning wood, of damp clothes and of cheese.

"Are you alone?" she asked, peering at the benches in the shadow.

"I'm alone. They've all gone to the big shed to sleep."

She crossed the high threshold and entered. Jasiek was sitting on a bench and warming his hands at the fire.

"Are you cold?"

"My hands are so cold I scarce can warm them."

"Why don't you warm them on Yadviga? She'd warm you fine and quickly."

Jasiek smiled mockingly, looked up at Krystka, who was standing by him and said quietly:

"Because I wanted to have a look at you too."

"But I don't want you," shouted Krystka. "Do you hear? I don't want you here."

"Then where?" smiled Jasiek. "In the big shed?"

The hot blood rushed into Krystka's face and tears glittered in her eyes. She caught him by the shoulders.

"Jasiek!"

He looked at her with phlegmatic irony, with stupid impudence and asked:

"What?"

Krystka fell on her knees before him. A branch that she knocked aside with her foot shot sparks up to the roof beam.

"Jasiek, I loved you, didn't I?"

"Oh, what has been has been," he replied, arranging with the blade of his mountain axe the burning brands on the hearth. The stirred up fire crackled and flamed up.

"Didn't I love you?" said Krystka, groaning rather than speaking. "Wasn't I true to you for three years past? You were my first and last. Didn't I nurse you, when Vavrzek Mientus cut your head open? Didn't I save you the time you were fallen upon at the wedding? Didn't I stop the police at the door, when they came to search because you'd stolen money in Hocholov? Still my body's blue from the blows of their musket-butts they gave me, while you climbed through the window at the back. Didn't I look for you, when you fell hunting chamois from the precipice on Mied-

[190]

ziany? You were nearly frozen to death. A Luptov
bullet nearly shot me then, Jasiek!

"What d'you want?"

"What have I for all that? What have I?
What?"

"Coral beads and twenty-five talars."

"If only I had them here, I'd throw them into
that fire."

"What's made you so mad?"

Here Jasiek took a pipe from his jacket pocket,
and began to clean it with a bit of wire and fill it
with tobacco.

Krystka, kneeling, put her arms about him and
her mouth close to his face.

"Jas, Jasiek," she said painfully, "Weren't you
happy with me those three years?"

Jasiek shook out the ash on to his palm, took out
tobacco, and made to fill his pipe.

Krystka looked into his eyes.

"Jas!"

"What?" asked Jasiek. He spat on to the tobacco and began to roll it between his hands.

"You won't go any more to her?"

"Where am I not to go?"

"To Yadviga. . . ."

Jasiek packed the pipe, put it to his mouth, took
a burning stick out of the fire, put it to the pipe

[191]

and pressed the tobacco down with his finger, and puffed two or three times. Then he threw the stick into the fire and spat into the flames. Krystka crouched beside him, and looked at him as a mother looks at her child.

"Jas," she said in a whisper, "I'll give you anything you ask for."

"Why, you've given me everything already."

"I'll look after you like a mother. You'll never have to do any work. . . ."

"I don't do so very much even now."

"You'll live like a lord! I'll cook meat for you every day."

"Will you indeed?"—and again Jasiek spit into the fire. "And what more will you give me?"

"I'll put up the banns."

"With whom?"

"Jasiek, don't be so cruel! You're like a devil."

Jasiek got up from the bench.

"Where are you going to?"

"Wherever I like," he said quietly.

Krystka caught him once more round the waist.

"Didn't I love you? Didn't I worship you? Didn't I caress you?" she said in a coaxing voice. "When you came to me I was yours. When you came by night and just tapped on the window or on the wall, didn't I open to you? If you came in the winter, however cold it might be, didn't I run

to you in my night clothes? Didn't I come bare-
foot? Like salvation I welcomed you! Jas!"

Krystka touched his knee with her forehead
and clasped his knees.

"Jasiek, Jas!"

But Jasiek had got a bit impatient: he pulled
away and made for the door. Krystka didn't let
go, so he dragged her along the ground.

"Let me go!"

"I won't. You're mine. You're mine. You're
mine."

"I'll be whose I like!" said Jasiek impatiently.

"I'll kiss your sandals. Don't you want me any
more?"

"Kiss them," retorted Jasiek. "You didn't buy
me, and you can't tie me up like a bullock."

"I bought you—and forever!"

"With what?"

"With my heart."

"Oh, stop it!" said Jasiek, and made for the door
again.

Then Krystka stood up suddenly and shouted.

"Stand still!"

Her voice was so furious, her eyes glared so that
Jasiek stopped in his tracks.

"Stand still!" shouted Krystka. "Tell me what
more you saw to like in that slut than in me? Is she
richer than I? She's a beggar! Is she fairer than I?

[193]

What made you like her more than you like me?
You never saw her before this summer and all at
once you wanted her. At once you shamed yourself. You did. How did she charm you? Tell me!
Am I not a girl worth looking at? Eh?"

She stood before him with her shawl fallen back
on her shoulders, her hair tousled, with her black
eyes glowing and her sunburnt face aflame.

Jasiek had his hat at the back of his head and his
pipe in his mouth, and he was leaning on his mountain axe.

"What did you see in her more than in me?"

"Her grey eyes."

"Grey eyes?"

"Aye."

Krystka's face flamed yet more, and it was as if
a thunderbolt hung between her dark brows.

"Her eyes?" she cried again.

"Aye," repeated Jasiek carelessly and impatiently.

The thunderbolt was still in its place; but
Krystka's face changed and her little, sharp teeth
showed between her lips as she smiled.

"So you don't want to go to her?"

"I'll go when I like."

"Certainly. Of course you will. If only I could
paint my eyes grey too! But I can't. They won't
turn grey for me. There's nothing that can be

[194]

done. But wait, Jas, don't go to her. I'll bring her here to you. When you spoke so sensibly to me I understood. Sit here on the bench in the shed, and I'll bring her to you at once."

She seized a big brand from the hearth.

"It's dark," she said. "I'll light my way."

Jasiek twisted round still leaning on his mountain axe and looked at Krystka, a little surprised.

"What are you going to do, Krystka?" he asked.

"I'm going to bring her to you. You shall have her here, in the shed."

"Krystka!"

"Sit there. In a moment we'll be here. When you spoke so sensibly to me, I understood."

With the blazing brand in her hand she ran out of the shed and Jasiek saw through the chinks that she ran towards Yadviga's hut, a few hundred paces away.

"Yadviga's lying in the shed," he thought. "Shall I call her to me or what shall I do?"

He sat down quietly again with his face towards the fire.

Krystka ran up to the other shed where Yadviga was. The bells of the cows that were shut up for the night jingled. Yadviga was sitting on the threshold.

"What is it?" she asked, seeing the fire from the brand coming towards her.

"Aren't you asleep yet, Yadviga?" asked Krystka.

"No. Is that you, Krystka?"

"Yes."

"Why have you come with that fire?"

"For you."

"Why?"

"Come with me."

"Whither? Whither should I go?"

"To Jasiek."

"To Jasiek? He'll come himself," retorted Yadviga.

Krystka was silent for a moment, then said in a strange voice:

"You have grey eyes, Yadviga."

"They are what they are. What is it to you?"

"Yadviga, you've grey eyes, haven't you?"

"Look at them, if you don't know."

"Show me!"

"Go away to where you came from. What d'you want with me?"

"Show me those eyes of yours!"

"Krystka! Are you mad? What d'you want?"

Yadviga twisted herself round as she sat until she looked Krystka straight in the face. The fire from the brand lit her up.

"What d'you want?"

"I want your eyes. That's what I want!" cried Krystka, and thrust the flaming brand into Yadviga's face.

A terrible shriek that shook the very mountains tore the woodland twilight, tore the night. Dogs barked fiercely. Echo sounded far into the distance, as if the crags were screaming round about. Another shriek followed, and another, and yet another. The whole clearing seemed full of that frightful, that heart-rending screaming.

Jasiek leapt from the shed and ran towards Yadviga's.

"What's happened?" he cried. "Confound it all, who's yelling like that. What is it?"

His voice died in his throat. Krystka held by the hand Yadviga who was shrieking and writhing on the ground. Above her a halo of sparks flew and whirled. Seeing Jas she cried:

"There she is for you. There are her grey eyes. Look at her!"

She beckoned to him with the brand.

"What have you done to her, you wretch?"

"What have I done? I've burnt out her eyes," laughed Krystka. She let go of Yadviga and threw the flaming brand far from her.

It became quiet and dark.

Then she went up to Jasiek, who stood motionless with horror, and put her arms round his neck, strongly, lithely, persuasively; and she bent his head towards her.

"Now you'll be mine," she said, in a wild half whisper. "Now you'll be mine!"

And he bent towards her, compelled but unresisting.

Krystka took his hand and drew him into the dark, whispering wood.

10.

HOW JOZEK SMAS
WENT TO CONFESSION

JOZEK SMAS SOLICARZ of clan Mrovca, from Olcha, was a mighty hunter but a still mightier robber, headstrong and inveterate, for he robbed not from need but because he loved to. But most mightily of all was he godless. When folk greeted him with: "May Jesus Christ be praised!" his answer was never other than "All right! All right!" or "Let it be so. I have no objection"— which didn't take him shorter but even longer to say than: "Forever and ever, Amen!" If, as a hunter he was the equal of Janek the Hungarian of Jurgov, who wasted the chamois from Havran through all Litvorova and even as far as Mount Koscieletz, if as a robber he equalled Janek of Brzezavitza of whom it was sung:

On a height they're raising a gallows-tree so tall:
Jan from Brzezavitza will hang before them all—

as to godlessness, he was Antichrist himself. And the strange thing about it was that, in spite of it, he was rich among the mountain sheep-farmers, every-thing went well with him, he had luck in all things. Misfortune found no way to him. Things went so well with him that it was as if God had purposely blessed him, and maybe he was never in church un-less it were when he was christened.

It wasn't that he didn't believe anything down to

"life everlasting, Amen," but that he didn't want to hear or know anything about all that.

"I don't see at all," he would say, "that the Lord God pushes Himself on me, so why should I bother Him? If I sow I reap; if I don't sow there'll be no grain. If I eat I'm not hungry; if I don't I am. I live, for I was born; I shall die for death will come. I know that the mountains aren't low, for I've gone over them. I know wood is hard for I've cloven it. I know that fire burns and water quenches—But I know of the Lord God only as much as I know of that king there, ruling somewhere in his chief city. I'm not the man to make haste towards anyone."

Sure of himself the fellow was, never at a loss and terribly bold.

In spite of that godlessness of his, folk loved him, for he was kind; he wronged no man, he helped folk when they were in trouble, he was wise and eloquent in counsel, and if he brought money home from anywhere he would treat all who willed till they were sated. To the inn where he liked to drink folk gathered, not alone from Olcha and Pardolovka and Hruby, but from Zakopane, from Poronin, from Murzasihl, from Cichy and from Bukovina, when they heard he had come there with his pockets full; and he rejoiced in that and, time and again, gave one the wherewithal to buy a cow or a horse or seed for sowing.

But luck favored him—and left him. He was no longer young, being about fifty-five, when, as he was hunting near the Frozen Pond, a storm surprised him, bringing wind, snow and frost. For three days and three nights he sat in the shelter of a rock, for he couldn't stir. It was so far well with him that he had a bit of food by him. He got home at last and illness crept upon him. Only now the smack of a bear's paw which he got near Rohacze before he could shin up a tree, made itself felt in his back. So, too, did the blow on his knee that a stone gave him in falling somewhere on Miller Mountain; and the broken rib in his side that he got from the men of Spiz near the five Hungarian Lakes, when they smashed him with their goat-sticks; and the holes in his head from his youthful fights. Something began to split his bones, to bore them, to break them. It was all he could do to bear it. He lost flesh, he got weaker, he could scarce leave his bed.

Neither bear fat nor marmot fat, whether swallowed or smeared on, did him any good at all.

A wise old woman came—Katherine Magierka of the Janik clan—and burnt herbs and amber by him—no use! Another gossip came, still older, Trzebunka her name was, and said a charm over him—no use! Not even Jacob Bednarz, who was a hundred years old, could do him any good, though Jacob had cured sheep, cows and horses by touching them.

And then the old neighbor women got together; they sat round about his bed.

"Eh, gossip dear, your time's at hand," said one.

"Heigh ho, neighbor, we can't help you anyhow any more."

"Nobody in the wide world can help you more, my dear, save death itself."

"Mind, gossip dear, one should think of one's soul!"

"Lest it be too late, neighbor!"

"But who knows—sometimes it happens thus— Perhaps after Holy Communion it would let go a bit."

"True indeed, you say well gossip. And what, good-man, if you went to confession?"

"Before the miraculous Mother of God at Ludzimir."

"Why, there's a miraculous one at Odrowonz, they say," suggested Smas, who liked the idea of Odrowonz better, because it was further off. 'Tis the nature of hunters and robbers to go far if they go at all.

"Oh, my dear man, she isn't fit to be a little cook-maid to the Ludzimir one."

"Go, neighbor, go, and confess!"

"Oh, go, gossip, go for it's urgent. Go, make haste, for it's high time!"

"Go, go, dear man!"

"The devil won't be able to get at you, and you know he'll not be far away now."

"That's true enough, gossip, 'tis wisely said. Not far, not far!"

"As I was coming from home yesterday, my dear man, a big, black cat leapt out from under my feet. I shrank back in a fright."

"The devil likes to change himself into a cat."

"Oh, my dear woman, he's been seen in a dog's skin too."

"But he'd rather change himself into a cat."

"What does it matter to such as he? He can do what he likes. The devil's the devil."

"When Simon Mrovca was in his death-agony, the devil showed himself as a wolf. Near, near, close by the cottage it passed."

"Terrible, terrible!"

"And by what did they know that it wasn't a real wolf?"

"Oh, those that recognized him knew all about it. They say fire came from his muzzle. 'Twas at night."

"Terrible, terrible!"

"And old Mrovca didn't make his confession?"

"They couldn't bring a priest to him in time. The horses stopped short in a snowdrift."

"There you are! 'Twas that wolf who did it, none other!"

"So all agreed, 'twas none other than he."

"Oh, sweetest Lord Jesus!"

"Mary immaculate!"

"All ye holy angels which are in heaven!"

"Gossip, gossip, go and confess! It's all up with you, that's easily seen."

"All up, all up! You've dwindled away. Half of you's gone. You're going all to nothing."

"Go, go, dear man, death won't let you off this time."

"Right enough, right enough!"

"Oh no!"

And when they began to groan and lament and whine over him, Jozek Smas made up his mind to drive to the Lord God in Ludzimir.

It was fixed he should go on the day of the "indulgence," the eighth of September, the very birthday of the Holy Virgin.

The rain, that had been pouring down all through August, stopped. Josek at once got better —his bones ceased to be broken and bored so terribly.

He got up out of bed, washed himself, smeared his hair with butter, put on clean linen, a new hat, a new coat, a new sheepskin jacket, trousers and sandals, as if for a wedding. The women who had urged him to go and were to go with him, were glad. He had no wife then, he was a widower. But how amazed they all were—for a cart drew up before the cottage, and in it were two fiddlers and a double-bass player—as if for a wedding! But folk opened their eyes still wider when Smas came out with two pistols and two knives in his belt, his axe in his fist and a flint-lock over his shoulder.

"What the devil, neighbor? Why, you're not going chamois-hunting!"

"Nor to Luptov to get money, dear man!"

But Jozek Smas leant on his long-handled axe and said: "Not otherwise did I go to meet any other Lord, be he Squire or Director or Cashier or Merchant, or anyone at all. And you say yourselves that the Lord God is the greatest of all. And though I'm going to Him on a different errand, I won't insult Him because He won't pay me as much as a squire or sheep-farmer or damned Jew, whom I went full-armed to meet. Let Him not feel hurt, let me do Him no wrong! And as we're to make it up, He and I, I'm taking music with me, so that He may know that I don't grudge money on our agreement, that I'm ready to pay. Let Him know that if He's the husbandman of Heaven, I'm as good a one any day at Olcha. Perhaps He'll thunder, then I'll bid my basses answer Him back. Oh ho!"

So he set off. On the front cart drove the band, playing. On the second, close behind, drove Smas with the old women.

Folk looked and wondered as he drove through the Novy Targ villages. At Zaskale the carts turned into the road that leads to Ludzimir. On and on they went. They had started very early, so they got there in good time. There were crowds of people, a great gathering for the Indulgence Day. There was noise, bustle, no room anywhere.

Anyone that looked at the cart all but crossed himself. There was the band driving in front, and behind an old fellow, gray-haired, with pistols in his belt, with the barrel of his flint-lock gleaming behind his shoulder and he looking boldly as an eagle does, though it was easy to see that he was ill.

"Goodness gracious, whatever is it?" one asked another. "Who can it be?"

"Someone from Podhale, one of those winged folk, or from Bukovina or Koscieliska," said others.

"He's got a gun with him."

"Maybe he's a gamekeeper from goodness knows where."

"But many a gamekeeper or even forester has come here and has no gun with him."

They wondered; they couldn't make it out.

Smas pulled up before the church.

The crowd was all about him. There were folk from Black and White Dunayec, from Shaflary, from Ostrovsk, from Pyzovka, from Vroblevska, from Podchervienny, from Koniovka, from Pienionzkovice, from Odrovonzh, from Ochotnitza, from Niva, from Lasek, from Klikushova, from Lopushna, from Sieniava, from Kraushov, from Rogoznik, from Dlugopol, from Marushyna, from Moravchyn, from Rabka, from Novy Targ, from the whole countryside and from further off—from Sucha, from Zyviec, from Vadovicza, from Myshlenitza and from further yet—from Spizh, from Kubin even, even from Hungarian Kiezmark. Thousands were there; but Smas from Olcha was notable among them all.

There wasn't much room in the church and priests were hearing confessions outside under the lime-trees in the churchyard. A young priest suddenly heard the band playing, for Smas kept forbidding it to stop, and he rushed out of the confessional, shook off the old woman he'd just finished hearing, leapt forward and looked about him—and then how he shouted at them!

[209]

Different things he called them. A lively priest was he!

The band stopped playing.

"Who are you there?" cried the priest. "What do you want here?"

Smas stepped forward—the old woman came behind him, the gossips. He took off his hat and said:

"I don't know how to speak to you: Sir, father, or what, for I'm not learned in that, I never had to do with it; for my church has been Mount Gierlak and my belfry the Icy Peak. But the women persuaded me. "Go to confession," said they, so I've come to confess. If you'll hear me, I'm ready."

The old women with him were horror-struck, for they'd been teaching him on the way what sins were and how one should confess and how to speak fitly to the clergy; and here was Smas talking in his own way—a robber's way!

The priest, too, opened his eyes wide at these words and the folk round about surged forward in a wave.

"Well?" asked Smas.

The priest bade him disarm.

"Is that your first order?" asked Smas. "And there I thought that I should come full armed! But be it as you will!"

He disarmed himself; he gave his weapons to the farm-boy who walked behind him.

The priest ordered the people back.

"Kneel down here!" he said to Smas.

Smas knelt down.

"I won't keep you long," said he, "for I see so many folk waiting. The gossips have been teaching me what sins are. Neither a bushel nor even a quarter have I; so listen!

"Rob I did, but I gave the poor of my booty. More than one have I hung so high that his head nearly came out above the trees, so tall he grew! But that I never did on our side of the mountains, only over in Hungary. Fought I have, but I never attacked a weakling. Once only a wretch, miserably small he was, came from the army and hit me on the head. Then—I beg your Reverence's pardon—I clasped him round the stomach and the neck, turned him upside down, stuck him in among the branches head downwards and went away. I wouldn't touch the thing!

"I've done no hurt to any animal, nor maimed one, except when hunting, but that's a hunter's right.

"No man have I defamed or betrayed; I've kept faith always, both when we robbed and hid the booty and when we agreed on a raid, and otherwise. I never wronged comrades either when the booty was divided or when we went marmot-hunting—nay, I have given of my share to comrades who were poor.

"Drunk I have, but no harm came of that—nay even, the innkeeper gained.

"Killed a man I have, but not needlessly—There! In the end it had to be, for fight they would! And you know yourself how it is—a robber hasn't much time to waste when he's robbing. I've forgotten if 'twas two or three that I killed—'twas so long ago.

"So many sins have I on me—a few, not many."

And what do you think happened?
Smas got well!
But he gave up his robber's trade.

"It wasn't so much what that little priest kept saying to me that got me," said Smas, "though he talked so finely to me about hell that it was a joy to listen; neither was it the penance he put on me, and there was a fine lot of it; it was that I got well.

"That little priest prated and prated what the devils were like there in hell, how they seeth souls in pitch, how they tear them with pincers, drag them over spikes—and all the time I kept thinking to myself: "Well, all kinds of things have been at me in my lifetime and I'm not so much afraid of those devils after death. I don't know if they're any fiercer fellows than the men of Spiz and though *they* had me in their hands I got out! You don't scare a highlandman, and a robber to boot, with devils! He's had to do with enough of the kind. A snowstorm comes on among the peaks, you're snowed up. The Luptov men of the Austrian guard come at you—aren't they devils?",

"But I kept thinking to myself: "If Thou'lt help me, Lord God, so that I get well, I'm Thy man!""

"And so it came to pass. Marmots' and bears' fat could do nothing—old women's and men's charms and enchantments nothing, and He, the Lord God, managed it! I'd said to myself when the little Father prated so masterfully, saying that the Lord God hates robbery: "If Thou dost cure me, Lord God, I'll go no more into Luptov, I'll kill no more, if Thou hast no pleasure in it, nay, if it even grieves Thee. Ho! If Thou'rt good to me, so I'll be to Thee." I was always like that. If I was out with a man, God forbid! It was as if flames ran over my hands. But if I was well with anyone or if we made it up, then I gave my word but once, like Him up there above the clouds."

11.

HOW WOJTEK CHRONIETS
WAS TAKEN

ITTLE Jacob Hucianski rushed at full speed up towards the mountains, shouting:

"Aye, indeed, I'll tell him! Aye indeed, I'll tell him!"

Little Jacob was fourteen and perfectly understood that nobody was to be told that Wojtek Chroniets, who had deserted from the Austrian army, was at their place in the upper pastures. But he also understood perfectly that Wojtek should be told that Kasia Penckowska, Wojtek's sweetheart, was dancing in the inn with the other fellows. And so he rushed upwards and shouted:

"Aye indeed I'll tell him! Aye indeed I'll tell him."

He also rushed upwards very fast because he was afraid of a bear, which the night before had "made meat" in the clearing.

The woods ended, the red firs began to get thinner, the clearing shone, flooded with moonlight.

"Here we are," said little Jacob to himself.

Then he began to call the dogs: "Here! Here! Here! Here!" and they, recognizing his voice, ran barking towards him. "Watch," as big as a calf, got under his feet, little Jacob straddled across him, caught him by the collar and amid a tremendous barking drew up on his back before the chief shepherd's shed.

"Oh, but you're quick indeed"—said the chief shepherd to him. "And did you bring everything?"

Little Jacob took out of his bag some packages of tobacco, pipes and tinder.

"Everything's there that you told me to bring."

"Here, take these," said the chief shepherd, giving him four copper coins.

At that very moment Wojtek raised himself heavily (he lay near the wall on a bench), put his hand into his belt and gave Jacob a silver twenty crown piece.

Little Jacob had noticed that there had come twice to Wojtek some stranger fellow, very tall, that they said something in a low voice to the chief shepherd and afterwards Wojtek was away, once only a night, a day, and a night, once something like four days; and after he came back he had a lot of silver money, twenty crown pieces, thalers, and even gold ducats. Of these he gave one each to two dumb men shepherds from Mur, the Hajaceks, Michael and Kuba; fellows each of whom could lift three hundredweight of iron with his teeth, and on his back even eight hundredweight. But they were quiet boys and did no harm to anyone. Besides Kuba, though dumb, could play wonderfully on the pipe, and on the long horn he played till echo repeated his playing.

Little Jacob had also noticed that Wojtek Chroniets did not bring that silver and gold from anywhere except from beyond the Tatra Mountains, from Liptow; and that big man could not be anyone else than an emissary of the robbers with whom Wojtek kept company.

But no word was said of that. Only little Jacob had remarked that the chief shepherd, his uncle, specially favored Wojtek, gave him the best bits, and sometimes he used to say: "You'll come to something some day, Wojtek! . . ."

Jacob knew too that Wojtek wanted to marry Kasia Penckowska, and she had even been twice with him on the upper pastures, for it was not convenient for Wojtek to go down to the village, on account of his position as a deserter from the Austrian army.

Little Jacob had also heard how she had sworn to Wojtek that she would stop going to the inn, that she wouldn't dance, especially with Bronislaw Walencak of Kosny Forge.

His heart was very indignant when, while buying the tobacco and tinder, he saw Kasia dancing a polka with that very Walencak; and not only did he see this, but also how in the crowd Walencak caught her round the waist and kissed her twice on the very mouth, and once on her cheek.

Little Jacob's heart was still more indignant when he felt Wojtek's twenty crown piece in his hand. So he stood before him and says:

"Wojtek, I'd like to tell you something!"

"What?"

"Kasia is dancing."

At that Wojtek sat up suddenly.

"She's dancing, is she?"

"She is."

"Where?"

"In the inn near the church."

"Did you see it?"

"I saw it."

"With whom?"

"With Walencak."

Wojtek sprang from the bench and stood on his two feet. He was barefooted and he trod a little on the sparks from the fire. But he paid no attention to that.

"Are you telling the truth?" he said, and caught little Jacob by the arm.

"I swear it's true!"

"Here, take this!" said Wojtek, and threw the boy a thaler; little Jacob put it away, then Wojtek sprung to the wall, seized his leather sandals, and put them on.

The two immense Hajaceks, sitting motionless on a very low bench near the fire, with their heads bent towards the flame, in black, tarry shirts, with brass-studded belts that reached up to their armpits, raised their heads and looked at each other. In their smoke-blackened and sunburnt faces shone only the bluish whites of their eyes.

Wojtek finished putting on his sandals.

"Where are you going?" asked the chief shepherd.

"There."

"Look out!" warned the chief shepherd.

"Don't be afraid. I'll come back towards morning."

"May the Lord guide you."

"May God be with you."

They shook hands.

Wojtek took his hatchet and went out of the shed.

The two immense, black Hajaceks rose heavily from the bench and nodded to the chief shepherd.

"Are you going with him?"

They bent their heads in assent.

"As you will."

The dumb men left the shed, taking down their hatchets which had been struck into the wooden wall.

"Why the devil did you tell him that?" said the chief shepherd, turning to little Jacob.

"How could I not tell him when I heard her

swear that she wouldn't dance? And he begged her most of all not to go with that Walencak."

"Ho! Ho! There'll be trouble there," said the chief shepherd half to himself, and raking out a clay pipe from among the small coal and ashes, he began to puff at it and sank into a reverie.

Wojtek rushed along so that the little stones and gravel sputtered under his feet. He ran across the clearing, he ran through the wood, he didn't hear the Hajaceks behind him. It was only on the road that he heard them. But he didn't even look round; he rushed on. He rushed into the village, hurried towards the inn, and looked through the window; Walencak was dancing round and round, while Kasia followed him, her arms akimbo. Walencak just then stood still before the musicians and sang:

If thou loved'st me Kasia, even as I love thee,
Every night together surely we should be.

And old Bart Hucianski, a very merry fellow, sang to him from the corner:

That is all she's asking, that is all she's praying—
That the sun his rising should be still delaying.

And everybody burst out laughing.

Wojtek came into the passage, and from there he came and stood in the doorway. The two Hajaceks followed him into the hall.

Somebody touched him.

"How are you, Wojtush?"

He looked round. It was Florian Francuz, an elderly, lean, little, ugly, rich fellow, who was immensely in love with Kasia; and having no chance of rivalling Walencak or Wojtek, had conceived a hatred for Walencak. If he couldn't get her, let Wojtek take her!

"Glad to see you," says Wojtek.

"Do you see what's going on there?"

"And what should be going on there?"

"Kasia dancing with Walencak."

"That's why I came here."

"Oh, by God Himself, Wojtush!"

"It'll be as it is to be."

"Here's my hand! If you want to drink for three days, drink. I'll sell a cow, I'll sell a horse, and you'll drink! Little Wojtek! My pet! On my soul, drink!!! And what devils are those, who came with you?"

"Shepherds from Mur. The Hajaceks. They're dumb."

"Oho! And they're big men, too! If I were like that! I'd settle Walencak myself."

"Don't be afraid, I can settle him, too."

"Oh dear, oh dear, Wojtush! Drink afterwards as much as you like! I'll sell my meadow in Oblas, I'll sell a field, I'll sell a house. Drink, Wojtush!

My pet! I couldn't, so you will take her. Take her, take her, take her! Vrrr!!!"

Here Florek Francuz growled like a dog till he foamed. He stuck his nails into Wojtek's palm and shook all over, standing first on one foot and then on another, like a cock does.

"Do you see her there?"

"I see her."

"They're kissing each other, they're hugging each other, they're pledging themselves! Wojtush, V-r-r-r!!!"

Here Florek Francuz bent his head and caught Wojtek's shirt-sleeves in his teeth.

"Wojtush!"

"What?"

"I'll hold all your children at the font. I'll leave my whole fortune to them. I'll be like a father to them!!!"

And he pushed him into the room. The two immense Hajaceks stole towards the door.

At that moment the fiddler's string broke. The dance was interrupted. Kasia saw Wojtek. She got terribly upset, and flushed red, though already red from dancing. She didn't know whether to go towards him or not. What could she say to him? At length she approached, stretched out her hand and stammered:

"Dear Wojtek? Is that you here?"

"It is," said Wojtek.

Walencak, drunk, heated, stood beside her. He, too, stretched out his hand to Wojtek.

"Are you well, brother?"

"I am."

They shook hands so that the bones cracked.

The fiddler drew his bow across the strings. Now he could play.

Wojtek swung off his hat before Walencak, bowed low to him, and kneeling on one knee, raised his head and said:

"Brother, yield me the dance."

Walencak shook his head insolently.

"No, brother!"

"Please yield it to me, brother!"

"No, brother."

"You won't?"

"I won't."

"I'll pay you three dances for it."

"I won't."

But Walencak was already standing before the musicians, and was singing:

Don't you try, young fellow, to lord it in this inn!
Better men will stop you, Sir, if you once begin.

And Wojtek Chroniets answered him, pretending to sing gaily:

[225]

Either I'll be slain here, or I'll slay instead:
For my hair is bristling all about my head!

Walencak stood still, and looked at the other.
Wojtek looked back at him. They looked and
smiled, as they threatened each the other with his
eyes till the sparks flew. The men already understood that something was going to happen. They
moved away, and gathered in groups. Already the
women had made for their men, to stand beside
them. They signed to each other that something
was afoot.

The music played on, Walencak danced. He
danced about to a lilting note, but somehow he
was ill at ease. He didn't want to end the dance, if
only for his malice and pride; and yet he stopped
before the musicians, and sang for the last figure,
in a hoarse voice:

See my chestnut bounding!
See, his hoofs are sounding
Far on the Orava road.

Oh, my heart is breaking!
Oh, my love is waking—
Speed I to my girl's abode!

He let Kasia slip under his arm and was about
to seize her round the waist and turn her in the air

for the finale. Then Florek Francuz nudged Wojtek in the side, and whispered to him:

"Little Wojtek."

Wojtek rushed forward, caught Kasia by the pigtail, wound it round his hand and flung her to the earth, so that it trembled. She didn't even utter a sound.

"You bitch! Where are your vows?" cries Wojtek, and kicked her in the chest.

Walencak went stupid, opened his mouth and his eyes. Then Staszek Penckowski, Kasia's brother, rushed up from the side with a shout: "Beat him! Kill him!" and caught Wojtek by the throat. Walencak, too, came to himself and went for Wojtek.

Five or six fellows, friends and relations, one with a stool, a second with a kind of pestle, a third with an earthen jug in his hand, pouring the beer on his own head, rushed towards Wojtek. But at this moment the people about the door were swept aside both ways like bran in the manger when a cow blows on it, and the two immense dumb men, black, and shining with their brass-studded belts, raised on high their arms, bare to the armpit, in their loose shepherd sleeves. As the hammers beat in the Koscieliska forge, rising noiselessly and falling with a crash, so did they raise their two fists soundlessly and so did they bring them down with a clatter on the heads of the folk. A groaning and screaming arose from the throng. The blue whites of their eyes shining, and guttural sounds coming from their throats, the Mur men kept throwing the fellows about like sheaves in a field.

It was well they didn't strike with their hatchets, for then, O Jesus, Mary!

But Wojtek was crushing with his knees Walencak, whom he had thrown on the floor. He held him fast by the throat and was choking him. His hatchet had fallen beside him.

The folk began to retreat and run out of the inn; the musicians had huddled together in a corner by the wall. The Mur shepherds were chasing the throng into the hall, and there was a freer space round Wojtek. Florek Francuz slid towards him and nudged him on the arm.

"Wojtush!"

Then he growled like a dog:

"Vr-r-r!!!"

Wojtek reached for the axe, stood up, measured his blow and crashed the back of it down on Walencak's head, so that the brain spurted out. He struck a second, a third, a fourth time, where the blow happened to fall.

And Florek Francuz at every blow jumped upwards, shrieking in an uncanny, hawk-like voice:

"Beat him! I'll pay you for every pound of him!"

Wojtek kept on beating.

In the corner Florek Francuz was squeaking: "Wojtush, Wojtush! He, he, he! . . ." as he jumped from one foot to another.

Suddenly Wojtek stopped beating his victim. He seized from the counter a bottle of brandy, put it to his mouth, and drank it all. Then he snorted and looked round him. Walencak was like a piece of meat, Kasia was trampled upon, wounded, suffocated, and crushed in the crowd. She lay in her blood on the ground. The musicians in the corner had no clear way to get out.

"Play!" shouted Wojtek to them.

"Play!" he repeated, and flung them a handful of thalers from his belt.

"Play on!" and he raised his hatchet.

The fiddler hastily tightened the peg, and drew his bow across the strings. Wojtek then stood before him, and sang:

Play for me, my Master, as well as you can play!
For when I'm dead, O Master, you can put your bow
   away.

He began to dance. His feet slipped in the blood. He kicked Walencak aside. The innkeeper, white with terror, had dragged Kasia away, and hidden her under a bench. With the blood dripping from their scratched and bruised faces, the two Hajaceks stood in the doorway, holding their hatchets against their shoulders. Florek Francuz was in a corner, skipping, shouting from time to time and whistling.

Wojtek danced on; then he stopped, and sang again:

Double basses are booming, fiddles too are squeaking,
While chains for ankles in the fortress they're seeking!

He danced again, but the blood was ebbing from him. He had got enough blows, too, in the battle. He was staggering now, but he sang yet again:

A gallows, a gallows of fir-wood they are hewing;
A maiden, a maiden has been my undoing!

Then he dropped on to a bench, and sat there.
"Innkeeper!" he called.
The innkeeper was shaking with fear.
"What are your orders, Sir Chief!"
"Give me paper, a pen, and that—whatever you call it, which you write with!"
"You mean ink?"
"Right. Ink. Quick. Here's to pay for it!" He threw him a thaler.
The innkeeper brought paper, ink and a pen.

"Write, sir, for I can't," says Wojtek.

The innkeeper dipped his pen in the ink.

"Write, sir, as I tell you":

"To the local chief of gendarmes at Nowy Targ. I, Wojtek Chroniets, of Sobuscyn, deserter from the first cavalry regiment, report that I have killed Kasia Penckowska, because of her unfaithfulness, and Bronislaw Walencak Borkowski, because he caught me by the throat; and I ask you to come and take me. They may come fearlessly, I shan't defend myself."

"Now sign my name, Wojtek Chroniets of Sobuscyn. Amen. Send it by a wagon, so that they may come soon from the town."

"And you, boys"—he turned to the Hajaceks— "Run away, so that they may not kill you here or catch you. There's a fine lot of silver in a bundle, and two little pots of brand-new twenty crown pieces, hid in the earth in the Cleft Valley, where water pours out from under a rock, two shot-lengths to the right from a withered mountain fir, and two and a half shot-lengths downward on the left. Divide them and throw a quarter of a pot to the chief shepherd, because he kept me through the summer. Go to the mountains!"

He stretched out his hand towards them. They embraced one another.

"Go, and God be with you!"

The dumb men looked upon him and went out.

"Innkeeper," says Wojtek, "Is she still alive?"

"Who?"

"Kasia."

"I don't even want to look. . . . There's so much blood!"

"Oh, she's dead, she's dead!" squeaked Florek Francuz, and burst into tears.

Then Florek threw himself on the ground. He began to beat his head against the floor, to tear his hair, to roll about, to writhe and to groan and howl in despair.

Wojtek Chroniets let his chin fall on to his chest and whispered:

"Sleep comes over me. . . ."

Then as if in a dream he hummed softly:

Oh, thou wind from the fields, wild wind from the high peaks sweeping,
When I catch thee and fly, o'er a hundred beeches I'm leaping,
Oh, thou wind from the fields, thou wind mid the grey crags waking,
When they hang me on high, do thou my halter be breaking.

His head sank still lower—and he slept!

12.

TOWARDS HEAVEN

THE dealer's Hanka—so-called because she was the orphan girl of dealer Jas's daughter Wikta—was crossing the Skupni foothills, and the wind was blowing so hard that it seemed as if she must be blown down into the Olczyska Valley. It was so cold that even though she had on a fairly warm jacket and a shawl, which was fairly warm, too, the freezing cold penetrated to her very bones. Snow-clouds piled themselves up and moved across the sky, and the sun showed through them here and there, as through a leaden-colored veil, dull and lifeless. The wilderness was all about, and the roaring of the wind was so great that it put fear into the heart, for it was as though all the mountains were groaning together.

Well, who knows? When the wind begins to blow, you'd think that all the dead that lie on the mountains were crying and complaining. And of these there are not a few, and no priest blessed them—their blessing came from a bullet, an axe or a bear's paw; or else they fell from a crag or were caught by an avalanche, or a flying bit of rock detached from the mountain-side hit them on the head and killed them. The mountains weren't made today, or humans yesterday. There are many who might groan.

But despite the terror of the place and the lateness of the autumn, and the snowstorm and the frost, the dealer's Hanka made her way onwards.

If any had met her he'd have crossed himself, for she moved like a ghost amid the falling snow. He'd have wondered what made her go up there into the mountains, into the ravines, into the roaring of the wind. Nobody lived up there, only fear dwelt there, growling at the intruder from every turning of the way. There death grinned and humans weakened and fell and their souls went from their bodies. . . . Turn back, fool, now or never! If you go on the snow will cover you, and only God above will know where you lie. Never again will you see the green grass or the yellow corn, or the blue water. . . . You'll lie like a stone under the snow, till in spring the eagles and owls tear you to pieces and bear your bones to the four winds, scattering them far over the earth. What makes you go up there, girl? In God's name, turn back!

That's what anyone who met her would have said, but there was none to meet her. The chamois-hunters had hung their guns on their cottage walls, save those of them who were spending the winter in rock shelters near the mountain meadows. None would go hunting in snow like that. They wouldn't dare, for foolhardy folk who tempt Providence, are often punished for their too great daring. And except for the chamois-hunters, nobody wanders about in the mountains in autumn.

But Hanka was glad of just that very thing. She was glad that none would ask her any questions, that in that dreadful wilderness she was alone.

For what was she doing there? She was fleeing. She was fleeing further and further, to death, to destruction. There was no anger in her heart, only cruel pain and grief. It was his fault—his, Woytek Mrowca's, Woytek Mrowca's of Olcha, none other's.

Hanka wasn't angry with him—she was only sorry, unspeakably sorry, inexpressibly! He had kissed her so often, had held her in his arms, had pressed her to him, had sworn that he'd marry her —until he had his way with her. And he had it because Hanka had fallen so much in love with him that he was the whole world to her, that she quivered from head to foot at the very sound of his voice.

But when Woytek Mrowca had his way, he soon tired of her, and when she spoke to him of marriage, he said: "What a fool you are to think I'd take a beggar like you. I'm a fine young fellow, a farmer's son. I've land that yields thirty bushels, I've horses and cows and sheep, and what have you? Just what you stand up in. I'll marry whoever I like."

He scorned her because she was an orphan; she had few relations, and those she had had scattered far and wide.

Pain, like a sword, pierced Hanka's heart.

"Woytek," she said, "a baby's coming."

"Well, it's your fault. . . ."

"It'll be your baby."

"How do I know that," said Woytek Mrowca. "You serve in a Jewish house. Maybe it won't even be a Christian."

Hanka nearly fell. She said nothing, not a word. She ran to the cottage where she served, to the kitchen; she threw her shawl about her and, not even looking to see if Woytek was there or had gone away, she took her way upwards, towards the mountains.

She had herded cows near the Caterpillar Ponds, serving a rich farmer named Stachon, and involuntarily now she tended thither. Her eyes told her the way, and her feet took her along it. It was there, too, that she and Woytek had fallen in love with one another, to Hanka's misfortune. He had been herding sheep there, a whole flock of them. He had more than fifty in his flock, all his own. Besides he had blue eyes, red cheeks, he was lithe as a fir-tree. You just simply had to fall in love with him.

From the slope at the bottom of Magora, Hanka looked at the shelters, standing black amid the snow. She stood still.

God, almighty and merciful! It had been well with her there, well! From these shelters she had been wont to go out with the cows, in company with Agnieszka, to go out beyond the Green Mountain, to near Koscielec, to near Mecha. The two girls had often lain down with their faces to the sun, and had sung. . . . And the sun had shone on the grass and trees so brightly that it was a joy to see. . . . On all sides cows—brown, black, brindled, rang their bells as they moved about and up there, high, among the foothills, Woytek's sheep showed white, and Woytek lay near them and sang—how often he sang:

Green plain, green plain, spread before me there—
Come, come, over it, maiden mine most fair!

to which she would answer:

There beyond the streamlet stands a handsome lad—
Were he mine, to fast each Wednesday I'd be glad.
I would fast on Wednesdays, on Fridays wouldn't
*   drink—*
If he were refused me, I'd kill myself, I think.

To that he sang back:

> *Fear not, fear not, Hanka, that I might betray.*
> *Me, if I deceived you, God would cast away.*

And again she would reply:

Woytek, Woytek, will not pass me by—
Woytek, grazing white sheep on the mountains high.

The other girls often sang:

Whom a girl's in love with, all may thus descry:
When he's far she's smiling, when he's near she's shy!

It echoed all over Mount Koscielec, and all the flowers smiled at it.

Or again, old Tomek Michalcyn played on the bagpipes in the shelter, and Woytek leaped to the dance. She, Hanka, was the only girl he danced before, inviting her to be his partner. But the others just simply devoured him with their eyes.

And in the evenings, and this was the nicest of all, when it was raining hard outside, everyone clustered round the fire in the shelter. A big log smouldered, the resinous pine-blocks sent up sparks, and Tomek Michalcyn began to tell stories. Then she would cuddle into Woytek's arms, as a refuge from dragons and witches, and he would put his arm round her and press her to him. And then her heart would beat so hard that it nearly jumped out of her breast. Sometimes, taking advantage of the shadows, he would press his lips to hers —and then the world went from her. . . . He was dearer to her than the stars, than the sun in the sky; when she said her prayers her thoughts wandered to him. Perhaps the devil had a hand in all that.

Almighty, merciful God, did it all happen or not? Had it been nothing but a dream in the night?

She made her way down towards the shelters—not by the path, for there was no trace of that, but over the snow.

There was the shed, where she had been wont to shut up the milch cows at night; there was the shelter where Woytek had been used to sleep—and there was the chief shepherd's shelter, where all had met together, where Tomek Michalcyn had told stories and strummed on the bagpipes.

She went on.

She passed the shelters by and turned toward the Green Mountain. Something urged her forward, impelled her. What was it? It was the terrible, poisoned sting of his words:

"Maybe it won't even be a Christian. You serve in a Jewish house." The words buzzed in her ears.

The wind blew harder and harder, till it took her breath away. The driving snow hid everything from her eyes. In the snow-filled twilight some chamois from the Lily Mountain ran towards her —one, two, three—Hanka reckoned five.

They ran past and disappeared into the driving snow. They never scented her, the wind carried the scent away, and they couldn't. Then they turned back and vanished into the snow-cloud, like ghosts.

Hanka involuntarily took the same way, and began to climb up towards the Lily Mountain.

Queer red lights, like sparks from a camp-fire, like will-o'-the-wisps, began to dance before her eyes. At first they were far off, then they got nearer and thicker and redder—they were like a rain of blood. The piercing cold penetrated her through and through, cold such as she had never known, although she was moving the whole time, and was tired. There was a queer singing in her ears, too, and a burning pain in her brain, as if somebody was driving a wedge into it. She stood still. Twilight, silence, the terrible wilderness were about her. Sometimes a crag or a mountain wall loomed up in the drifting snow, but she couldn't be sure if they were really there, or if they only seemed to be. It was as if the snowstorm had enveloped the whole world.

Close at hand she could only see the frozen, white bushes of the knee-timber, into which the wind drove drifts of powdery snow. From time to time the sun gleamed out over the mountain, as if through a leaden-colored veil, dull and far off.

"Who knows what kind of a baby it'll be, if it'll be a Christian"—Hanka went on again.

"I've suffered, oh, I've suffered," she thought, "suffered enough for a whole world of folk. . . . I've been alone in the world since I was a child, in service. I was cold and hungry, I was beaten. . . . Everybody ill-treated me. And when by God's will I'd grown up, and they couldn't have ill-treated me so much, this happens! Oh Lord, oh Lord! Oh Lord, oh Lord! . . ."

Thus lamenting, she struggled upwards through the snow.

"Where am I going to?" she asked herself.

"Straight before me," she answered herself.

"To death?"

"To death!"

Once again came that burning pain in her brain, but worse than it had been before. At the same time she seemed to hear bells ringing afar off, and the priest singing as he'd done at her mother's funeral, when she was being let down into the grave. Something within her began to ask: Are you here or there? Are you at your mother's funeral or on the way to the Lily Mountain?

"Is there anything before me?" she thought. "Is there any village up there, are there any people?"

She stumbled, it got dark before her eyes, there was a rushing sound in her ears, like the sound of the wind among the rocks. She began to stagger, to sway to the left and to the right, and everything round her, crags and mountain walls, began to flicker and stagger and topple towards her. The snow-cloud, the mountains, began to crush her, to bend her. She felt as she had once felt on Indulgence Day, in the church at Ludzimierz, when there were thousands and thousands of people. The Mother of God stood there on the altar, with a golden crown on her head and the Lord Jesus in her arms. She had a blue cloak and a rosy face, and there were stars under Her feet.

"Hail Mary, full of grace, the Lord is with Thee—" began Hanka in a whisper.

As she did so a kind of brilliance hovered over her in the gathering twilight, a pale brightness that seemed to be dulled by the snow.

Hanka quivered. What was that over there?

The light grew distincter and came nearer, but still seemed to be dulled, enveloped in the snow that whirled about it.

Hanka was frightened and stopped. She spread out her arms and leaned backwards, and her mouth opened wide in terror, and the cold, moist snow drove into it. Fear took away her power of thinking, and her heart died within her, and then from that brilliance there came a soft and very sweet voice:

"Hanka, don't be afraid!"

Hanka shook from head to foot, and the voice went on:

"Come!"

"Whither?" whispered Hanka.

The voice answered:

"Towards Heaven!"

And amid the brilliance and the snow-mist there gleamed something like a golden crown and a blue cloak and blue eyes and a rose-blush face—pale, scarcely visible.

"Is it You, Queen of Angels?" whispered Hanka.

But no voice answered, only the brilliance began to advance towards the Lily Mountain.

Hanka followed it.

New strength seemed to have come to her. There was no longer a rushing in her ears, and the cold hurt her less. She plunged through the snow-storm, moving toward the Lily Mountain.

But soon again she began to stumble, red sparks began to fly before her eyes, there was a roaring in her head, and such a weakness came over her that she could scarcely put one foot before another.

"Lady, I'd like to sit down," she whispered.

"Sit down, then," replied the soft voice from the brilliance.

Hanka sat down under the shelter of a big rock, which sheltered her a little from the wind, she leaned against it, and stretched out her legs. But the brilliance dissolved somewhere into the snow-cloud and disappeared.

"Where are you, Lady?"

But nobody answered out of the snow-laden twilight. She wanted to cry out—she couldn't.

Great weights seemed to weigh down her hands and feet, and shivers to pass through the very marrow of her bones. She began to pant, she could no longer see, she could no longer hear. In her brain there was a dreadful void, a red, a flaming void. She felt the snow falling upon her, wet, ceaseless, covering her knees, her breast, her shoulders, her face? She got warmer—it was stifling—and then she began to feel sleepy.

"I'll go to sleep," she thought.

Then the whole world got dark, and the wind rushed from the Middle and Border Peaks, rushed with a frightful howling, chasing before it clouds of sharp particles of ice and immense snow-flakes like grouse's feathers, falling as an eagle carries it away. A very whirlwind of snow was about Hanka, it drifted upwards over her, warm blood began to flow from her face and neck, that were cut by the particles of ice.

"Death!"

The thought flashed upon her, and such terror clutched her that she would fain have jumped to her feet, have fled.

"Down! Down! To the village! To men!"

But she no longer had strength to rise. With a last effort, she tried to stand up and failed.

A groan of terror, of despair, of insane horror,

burst from her, and her fingers began convulsively to dig the snow.

"Save me! Save me!"

Then on the snow-cloud, in the dim, all-pervading twilight, the pale brilliance fluttered, scarcely visible, but seeming near, close above Hanka's head. And in the midst of that brilliance she could see as it were a golden crown, and beneath it a face like honey, and eyes like flowers. And it even seemed to her as if a hand touched her shoulder.

And out of the snow-cloud, and from this fleeting form, there came a soft, sweet voice:

"Come!"

"Whither?" whispered Hanka.

"Up to Heaven. Give me your hand!" said the Mother of God.

And Hanka gave Her her hand, and went.